HD
45
.F357
2002

HWBI

W9-AXM-760

Whoever makes the most mistakes wins : t

More Praise for
Whoever Makes the Most Mistakes Wins

"It's difficult to imagine a subject more compelling to most human beings than success and failure. Farson and Keyes present a refreshingly original point of view on the subject that illuminates a paradox and challenges our assumptions about how to tell one from the other."

—MILTON GLASER, PRESIDENT, MILTON GLASER, INC.

"Truth always seems to come in small paradoxical packages. This delightfully readable package by Farson and Keyes brilliantly fuzzes the frontier between success and failure, and thus reveals the fusion of opposites as the essence of truth."

—HARLAN CLEVELAND, PRESIDENT EMERITUS,
WORLD ACADEMY OF ART AND SCIENCE

"*Whoever Makes the Most Mistakes Wins* promises to become a classic in the genre of modern wisdom literature that includes Eric Berne's *Games People Play* and Laurence J. Peter's *The Peter Principle*. Its unexpected turns, liberating humor, and shrewd observations about social creativity and business innovation have the flavor of Mark Twain mixed with Zen and Taoist ribaldry. This is a wonderful book!"

—MICHAEL MURPHY, FOUNDER, ESALEN INSTITUTE,
AND AUTHOR OF *GOLF IN THE KINGDOM*

"As we move into the twenty-first century, an age of increasingly revolutionary technological advances, the concepts of success and failure must be reinterpreted and transcended if we are to be truly innovative in our ideas and discoveries. Richard Farson and Ralph Keyes provide an insightful and original examination of these concepts and of the critical need to redefine them in the postmodern world."

—RICHARD C. ATKINSON, PRESIDENT, UNIVERSITY OF CALIFORNIA

"Fabulous! I love this book. It's like a Zen koan: concise, wise, inspiring, and instructive. It is a modern guidebook for how to embrace paradox and free yourself from fear of failure. In a time when we're subjected to a host of irrelevant, sappy, or overly simplistic self-help books, this book provides intelligent, truly useful advice."

—MARY BOONE, PRESIDENT, BOONE ASSOCIATES, AND AUTHOR OF *LEADERSHIP AND THE COMPUTER* AND *MANAGING INTER@CTIVELY*

"As one who has led a large association with many employees, I wish I had had this book years ago. It is timely and something every reader will find helpful at the personal, interpersonal, and managerial levels. This is a rare 'must read' book that is also easy to read."

—HORACE B. DEETS, FORMER EXECUTIVE DIRECTOR, AMERICAN ASSOCIATION OF RETIRED PERSONS

"From my perspective in the field of art and design, the 'lucky mistake' is often the uncredited key to any significant breakthrough. In their new book, Farson and Keyes introduce the business world to the designer's most secret ally."

—JOHN MAEDA, ASSOCIATE PROFESSOR OF DESIGN AND COMPUTATION, MIT MEDIA LABORATORY

"Richard Farson and Ralph Keyes have hit on something big with this book. I say that as a man with a large and embarrassing pile of mistakes littering the road behind him. The fact is that some of those screw-ups hurt, some even kicked off a crisis, but *all* of them helped me in life. Failure is to success as a second wing is to a bird. You need it and so does he. It is unlikely either of you will fly without it. Pick up this smart, influential book and find out how those mistakes you've made, the ones you thought crippled you, can work to your advantage."

—AMBASSADOR RICHARD CARLSON, FORMER DIRECTOR-GENERAL, VOICE OF AMERICA, AND FORMER PRESIDENT AND CEO, CORPORATION FOR PUBLIC BROADCASTING

"This is a valuable book for just about anyone in our competitive world. The authors make a clear case for understanding that failing precedes almost all great wins in our society, and that tolerance, if not love, of failing creates the most successful environment. There are many interesting anecdotes and arguments throughout this most persuasive book."

—JANE ALEXANDER, ACTRESS, AUTHOR, AND FORMER CHAIRMAN,
NATIONAL ENDOWMENT FOR THE ARTS

"This book is a great read—interesting and enjoyable. Its title can be taken literally—whoever makes the most mistakes will, in fact, win. I think most successful managers reach the same conclusion, but late in their careers. Farson and Keyes have finally explained this successful style of management, one many of us have observed. I certainly hope their message reaches the business schools, so graduates can start off on the right foot. Where were they when I needed this book?"

—RAYMOND ALDEN, FORMER PRESIDENT, SPRINT

"This book is a welcome antidote to the numbing conventional wisdom about what constitutes corporate success and failure. It shows how to make the business environment both vital and humane."

—RICHARD POLLAK, CONTRIBUTING EDITOR, *THE NATION*, AND AUTHOR OF
THE CREATION OF DR. B: A BIOGRAPHY OF BRUNO BETTELHEIM

"In an age where everyone is looking to win with simple formulas, it is so refreshing to have a more thoughtful and wise discussion of what *winning* and *losing* really mean, and how *learning* is more important than either one."

—EDGAR SCHEIN, SLOAN FELLOWS PROFESSOR OF MANAGEMENT EMERITUS,
MIT SLOAN SCHOOL OF MANAGEMENT

Whoever Makes the Most Mistakes Wins

The Paradox of Innovation

Richard Farson and **Ralph Keyes**

*f*P

THE FREE PRESS

New York • London • Toronto • Sydney • Singapore

THE FREE PRESS
A Division of Simon & Schuster, Inc.
1230 Avenue of the Americas
New York, NY 10020

Copyright © 2002 by Richard Farson and Ralph Keyes
All rights reserved, including the right of reproduction
in whole or in part in any form.

THE FREE PRESS and colophon are trademarks
of Simon & Schuster, Inc.

For information regarding special discounts for bulk purchases,
please contact Simon & Schuster Special Sales:
1-800-456-6798 or business@simonandschuster.com

Designed by Paul Dippolito

Manufactured in the United States of America

10   9   8   7   6   5   4   3   2   1

Library of Congress Cataloging-in-Publication Data
    Farson, Richard Evans, 1926–
        Whoever makes the most mistakes wins : the paradox of
    innovation / Richard Farson and Ralph Keyes.
            p.   cm.
        1. Technological innovations. 2. Success in business. 3. Success.
    I. Keyes, Ralph. II. Title
    HD45 .F357 2002
    658.4'09—dc21   2002019861
    ISBN 0-7432-2592-9

For my grandchildren,
John, Page, and Savannah
—Richard Farson

For Gerry Cohen, who has
always supported me, even
when I made mistakes
—Ralph Keyes

Contents

Acknowledgments

We would like to acknowledge help from the following people:

For ideas that contributed to our own thought processes: Carlos Campbell, Michael Crichton, Dawn Farson, Hallock Hoffman, Doug Land, Kate Ludeman, Jim O'Toole, Edwin Nystrom, Alex Soojung-Kim Pang, Charlton Price, John Shlien, Jim Skelly, Hall Sprague, Andrea-Lawrence Stuart, and Susan Waitley.

For helpful critiques of an early version of the manuscript: Andrea Adkins, Lou Heckler, and Robert Scherer.

For acute editing: Noel Greenwood and Burton Beals.

For encouragement and helpful suggestions, including the suggestion that we write this book: Margret McBride, the agent who represented it.

For capably shepherding the book to publication: our editor, Fred Hills.

Introduction

What if your concepts of success and failure were to change dramatically? Suppose the paths to either turned out to be completely different from those you'd been shown? Imagine not even being able to distinguish one from the other, and entertain the idea that succeeding or failing is not the be-all and end-all of management.

Today, nearly every act of management is put to this test. Did it succeed or did it fail? It's the wrong test. The nonstop innovation that organizations need to navigate a changing economy involves at least as many so-called setbacks as it does apparent victories. In a rapidly changing economy, you are likely to confront as much failure as success. Does that mean you will have failed? Only on your grandfather's terms. A new world calls for fresh concepts. As competition gives way to "coopetition," and intellectual capital rivals financial capital, new ways of doing business are necessary. Redefining success and failure is an essential part of that process.

When ingrained attitudes about success and failure change, the meaning of every act of management changes, too. Changing those attitudes is not easy. At first, the idea that success and failure are not what we thought they were can be unsettling. Ultimately, however, it can be encouraging (as in being more courageous), freeing us to take bolder steps in life. Many already have, especially the entrepreneurs who see their failures as footsteps on the path toward success.

The hardest practices to change are those we take for granted. It's the things that "everybody knows" that get us in biggest trouble. What we know for sure stands in the way of what we need to learn, and keeps us managing with outmoded tools. A world in which change is the only constant can't be navigated with tried-and-true approaches. These approaches encourage us to drive confidently into the twenty-first century at the wheel of a Studebaker.

So it is with success and failure, as we usually use these words. When it comes to the revolutionary changes demanded by the evolving economy, these outmoded concepts serve little purpose. Today's most creative innovators realize that operating on the basis of yesterday's notions of success and failure only hamstrings and slows them down. *Relying on conventional, outmoded ideas about success and failure stands in the way of your ability to innovate, compete, and stay ahead of the curve in a changing economy.* That is the key message of this book. We hope it will help you manage better by challenging conventional assumptions about success and failure, sometimes turning them upside down, and, in doing so, discover new ways to manage that transcend them both. By the time you get to the last chapter, perhaps you will begin to wonder whether these terms belong in your leadership vocabulary at all.

1 · The Success–Failure Fallacy

One must be God to be able to distinguish successes
from failures and not make mistakes.
—Anton Chekov

A management consultant wrote a brief bio for his thirtieth college reunion. In it, he included the usual information: work, family, achievements. By most measures, this man was unusually successful. He was the father of thriving children, head of a respected think tank, and author of a best-selling book. After reviewing his paragraph, however, the consultant realized that it read more like a resumé than an honest report to his classmates. "Why would I write such a stilted, half-true account of my life for friends who knew me when?" he asked himself.

As a lark, the consultant decided to write a longer, more candid report about what his life had actually been like. It began:

Because I didn't receive a single "A" in college, I couldn't get into medical school. Instead, I worked as a lifeguard, but got fired at the end of the summer. My next job, selling advertising in the Yellow Pages, was interrupted by breaking my leg badly while skiing. This gave me three months to think about what to do with my life. Since I'd enjoyed my psychology courses in college, I thought I might try to become a school psychologist. So, I enrolled at UCLA to pick up psychology and education courses, but got kicked out of student teaching because I couldn't get along with my supervisor. Back to lifeguarding. Then I noticed that a prominent psychologist was giving a summer seminar at my alma mater, so I quit my job and enrolled. This experience was electrifying. The psychologist invited me to study with him at the University of Chicago. I was so intimidated by that most serious academic institution, however, that I put off going there for a year. Just before receiving my Ph.D. from Chicago, I was given a one-year fellowship on the Harvard Business School faculty. I left there at the end of the year with almost everyone mad at me.

The report went on like this for several paragraphs. Far from being a description of a smooth, upward trajectory, it portrayed a jagged course of life events. Failures mingled with successes, triumphs with setbacks. The consultant's full bio was a litany of opportunities seized, others blown, jobs taken, jobs lost, personal rebuffs, standing ovations, love affairs, marriage, divorce, remarriage, making *Who's Who,* getting fired, starting a think tank, making money, going broke, having a heart attack, learning piano, publishing books . . . and on and on. His failures led to successes and successes to failures. The two were so interdependent that it wasn't always clear which was which. So it is in most lives.

Tangled Line

Whose life can be located precisely on the map of success and failure? Sometimes, what seems to be a success at one point proves to be a failure at another. Premature promotions set one person up for a fall. Getting fired forces someone else to start a profitable business. A marriage made in heaven can't survive hellish periods. A rotten first marriage propels both partners into terrific second ones. Life-threatening illnesses can jolt survivors into living more fully. ("Best thing that ever happened to me!")

We like to think you either succeed *or* fail. Most situations are more ambiguous, however. So are most people. He's a success, we say. She's a failure. On whose terms? At what stage of life? How can we be so sure? Winston Churchill, after all, was considered by many to be a pompous failure until he became prime minister of Great Britain during World War II.

We're too quick to call someone or something a "success" or a "failure" when the jury is still out (which is true in most cases). These two are simply not that easy to sort out, untangle, tell apart. All they are is labels we hang on complex events trying to simplify them. What we usually end up doing is oversimplifying them. When we win and when we lose can be utterly dependent on circumstances, timing, the economy, even shifts in the public mood.

Remember Edmund Muskie? When he ran for vice president in 1968, Maine's Lincolnesque senator was considered the most impressive member of either ticket. Four years later, he was the leading candidate in the Democratic presidential primaries. Then, on a snowy day in New Hampshire, Muskie choked up while protesting press attacks on his wife. Televised images of the senator from Maine tearfully addressing a rally with snowflakes clinging to his eyebrows horrified American viewers. We didn't want a crybaby in the White House! That single incident scuttled Muskie's political career. He had "failed."

Fast forward twenty-eight years. Al Gore's campaign for president was floundering. The knock on him: He was too stiff, too wooden. Gore's feelings were stored in a lockbox. He never got misty-eyed, like—well—like Ed Muskie!

In a different time and place, Muskie's catastrophic failure might have been considered a roaring success. If Maine's senator had been campaigning in the age of Oprah, his tearful outburst might have won him plaudits. Muskie would then have been viewed as a devoted husband and passionate candidate who could communicate soulfully with the American public.

Failure and success can be utterly dependent on such intangibles. Luck happens: good and bad. The fabulously wealthy J. Paul Getty said his success formula was "Rise early, work late, strike oil." As Getty realized, success or failure in business can have little to do with anything done by design. On a given new project everything might seem to be in place, ducks all lined up, every detail checked out. Then, some unexpected meteor lands on that project. A well-designed SUV might be launched just as soaring gas prices revive demand for more fuel-efficient vehicles. A surefire best-seller gets published right after *New York Times* reporters go on strike, taking its best-seller list with them. Or things might break the other way. A chance encounter at a class reunion leads to a big contract. The unexpected failure of a competitor opens new markets for your product. If the inventor of a computer operating system called CP/M had accepted IBM's invitation to pitch his product rather than go on vacation, Bill Gates might be a small-time Seattle software merchant rather than the developer of MS-DOS (which IBM bought instead) and one of the world's richest men.

Now we all can agree that Gates did succeed, big time—right? Well, not everyone. It took Mary Gates years to reach that conclusion. Long after Microsoft was flourishing, Mrs. Gates considered her son Bill a failure because he had dropped out of Harvard. Traditionally, that's what dropouts have been considered: failures. In the midst of an economic revolution led by college dropouts such as Bill Gates and Steve Jobs, however, this attitude is changing. As Mary Gates eventually conceded, leaving college—even Harvard—may simply reflect a shift in priorities.

Says Who?

Success, failure: Who's to say? These are much more ambiguous concepts than is suggested by success seminars, management texts, or performance reviews. The terms defy definition. Each one of us has a concept of success as unique as our fingerprints. Appearances aside, it's rare for anyone to achieve every measure of success as he or she may define that word. Despite what is written in annual reports and Christmas newsletters, unqualified success and clear-cut victories are rare. Most lives include few pure successes—or failures. Most must be qualified one way or another. That's why people who *appear* successful seldom *feel* successful. They know that what others perceive as their success is more of a mixed bag and, to some extent, undeserved.

Take Maria Shriver. If ever a woman would seem to have it all, it's Shriver. She's wealthy, attractive, has a movie-star husband (Arnold Schwarzenegger), four healthy children, a thriving TV career, and best-selling books on her resumé. Yet Shriver continually uses the word *failure* when discussing herself. What stands out in her mind is a single setback: when the version of CBS Morning News she hosted was canceled. And her many successes? Shriver brushes them off as a result of having big hair, impressive teeth, and, especially, being John F. Kennedy's niece.

In most lives, successes and failures are as tangled as fishing line after a bad cast. Failure begets success followed by failure and success once again. When we look back on our lives, the parts that once seemed triumphant can pale in significance, while episodes that appeared trivial at the time now look crucial. Successes, we see in hindsight, made us complacent, while our setbacks pushed us.

Country singer Joe Diffie said that the best year of his life was the one in which he lost his job at a foundry, got divorced, totaled his pickup, and was audited by the IRS. With so little to lose, Diffie left Oklahoma for Nashville, where he eventually became the Country Music Association's male vocalist of the year. "If the foundry hadn't been shut down," Diffie later admitted, "I'd probably still be there today."

As Diffie discovered, failures sometimes pave the way for successes and vice versa. We do everything we can to court triumph and hold adversity at bay, then find that unavoidable setbacks blaze the trail for our significant successes. Misfortune forces us to discover new paths to achievement, which, in turn, produce more setbacks and subsequent achievements in an endless cycle.

This is true in the lives of people and businesses alike. In the 1950s, it was thought that the success of television would lead to radio's demise. Instead, radio reinvented itself as a talk-show drive-time medium and roared back stronger than ever. Far from wiping out the market for fresh produce, as was feared, frozen vegetables whetted our appetite for fresh ones in countless new varieties. Convenience foods fueled a renaissance in gourmet cooking. Fast food inspired a passion for leisurely dining. The impersonality of web commerce will almost surely spark a renaissance of person-to-person selling at brick-and-mortar stores.

Why Success Resembles Failure, and Vice Versa

Winning and losing, victory and defeat, success and failure—all these concepts are far less clear than we usually imagine. Just when we think we know their meaning, it slips through our fingers. The harder we look at them, the fuzzier they become. Under close scrutiny, failure and success are hard to distinguish. One is the woof, the other the warp of a tightly woven fabric. Trying to tell them apart is like trying to identify the individual strands of an expensive rug.

What we usually regard as success and failure can be so similar that they defy distinction. Sometimes the two even resemble each other. They are like fraternal, if not identical, twins. That's not how they're usually perceived, of course. Success and failure have traditionally been treated as members of different tribes. One's a Viking, the other a Pygmy. They're opposites, like day and night, wet and dry, short and tall. Or so we like to think.

Westerners tend to think in absolutes. If it's hard, it can't be soft. If it's cold, it can't be hot. You're a winner or a loser. To succeed, you mustn't fail. Opposites, in other words, can't coexist. Eastern thought is more relaxed on this point. It embraces paradox: yin-yang, sweet and sour, the symbol of crisis embracing opportunity. Such concepts accept seeming contradictions as normal. In an increasingly complex world, we might be wise to follow the Eastern example.

There are compelling reasons to avoid making facile distinctions between success and failure. Assuming that they're opposites and, therefore, unrelated, is a fallacy. Nothing is so similar as opposites: love and hate, fear and longing, dread and desire. Laughing segues easily into crying. Scalding and freezing water sting in much the same way. Scratching an itch is not pain followed by pleasure, but both at once. Success and failure, too, have much in common. They don't necessarily duel to death. Sometimes, these two dance. One leads, the other follows, although it's not always apparent which is which, and who's doing what. Rather than coming from different tribes, success and failure are kin. Each contains genes of the other. The pollen of failure fertilizes the stamen of success. Together they produce hybrid vigor.

In simpler times, distinctions were easier to make. Gender roles were clear: Men held jobs, women kept house. Businesses with strong bottom lines were successful. Those that lost money were failures. Today, however, companies are judged as much on future prospects as they are on current performance. Profitability isn't always equated with success. Even stable corporations with solid profit-and-loss statements may be seen by investors as failures in the making. Today's hot company is tomorrow's iceberg. Overnight, fickle consumers turn their backs on products they had made into big hits. Word processing programs that were state of the art just a few years ago—XyWrite, WordStar, DisplayWrite—are museum pieces today. Hayes Modems set an industry standard (Hayes Compatible), then disappeared. After defining a fashion genre, Starter jackets went bankrupt. Success is a moving target, as are its symbols. What stood for success yesterday may represent failure today, and vice versa.

Can you imagine Steve Jobs and Stephen Wozniak taking a break to read *Dress for Success* while wiring the first Apple computer? Try to picture Bill Gates consulting the book *Success!* when launching Microsoft. Michael Korda's 1977 book featured drawings that illustrated do's and don'ts for conveying the image of a winner. One pictured The Loser's Jacket Pocket. This pocket held three pens and a glasses case. The nerd look, in other words. At the very time that his readers were studying how to avoid looking like a loser, Korda's loser look was common among those who eventually enjoyed the most success of all—on the author's own terms. A company like Microsoft was chockablock with employees who, to all appearances, were hopeless losers. A 1978 picture of Microsoft's eleven scruffy founders that's posted on the Internet is labeled, "Would you have invested?"

In a rapidly changing business environment, it's futile to try to stay abreast of symbols of success: the suits, ties, shoes, watch, pen, desk, and corner office that make one *appear* successful. Some of our most dynamic companies and those who work there shun those symbols. Yesterday's notions of success and failure have gone the way of gray flannel suits. In today's business climate, the concept of success has become vague, complicated, even contradictory. Measures of success and failure are more ambiguous than ever, part of the broader complexity of a global, digital, online economy.

To cope with this economy don't flee from its complexity; embrace it. In the world to come, we will repeatedly face fluid, ambiguous, even paradoxical, situations. Wisdom consists of realizing that every seeming paradox, all apparent contradictions, can't be resolved. Some even contain seeds of necessary change.

Many paradoxical notions are already floating about today's business world: Grow your business by destroying your business; to get big, think small; increase your share of markets by ignoring the concept of market share. We would add: Manage success and failure by not making clear distinctions between the two. How? Rather than trying to hang a label on every act—one reading SUCCESS or FAILURE—recognize that most situations contain elements of each. It's not success *or* failure but success *and* failure. When it comes to this issue, *both/and* is a far more useful concept than *either/or.* We can't cleave these two so cleanly, and shouldn't try. Using success and failure as a yardstick limits our ability to create, innovate, and take risks, which is the only way to stay afloat in the emerging economy.

Failure Pride

At the cutting edge of today's economy, creative minds have already embraced the symbiotic nature of success and failure. A more relaxed attitude toward both is routine among innovators throughout the country. Failure, they say, is "a step on the road to success." Some consider setbacks a badge of honor, unmistakable proof that they're bold risk takers. Far from hiding their blunders, they brag about them.

Attitudes toward success and failure are a fault line dividing generations. For any number of reasons, younger cohorts find the prospect of going belly up less daunting than their predecessors did. Partly, it's simply that they have less to lose by taking chances. Partly it's because they've known only affluence (the Depression to them is the subject of black-and-white documentaries on public television). It's also due to an attitude shift, however. These new workers realize—as a few thoughtful people always have—that pursuing success is like chasing the horizon, and that failure is an integral part of an interesting life.

Organizations that don't accommodate this shift in attitude risk losing some of their best, most innovative employees. Trying to retain them with the usual lures of salary, benefits, and perks won't work. Tweaking compensation packages accomplishes little when it comes to attracting and retaining innovators. This hardly means they don't care about money. Symbolically, it's terribly important as a way of keeping score. Money keeps you in the game, but it's the game that matters, not income as such. They would rather be given challenging assignments than get paid a premium to do routine tasks well.

Consider what so many younger employees do for relaxation: climb rocks, raft rivers, bike mountains, surf waves, trek in distant locales. In such activities, the risk of wiping out is a large part of the appeal. At work, they disdain "success" for the same reason that they go bungee jumping: as a flight away from security and toward adventure. So many come from sheltered backgrounds that the prospect of excitement entices them more than the security of a good salary. Stock options get their attention better than pension plans do. You might say they're starved for daring, suffering from risk hunger. It's no coincidence that their leisure activities stress challenge and sneer at luxury.

Winning and losing isn't what they're all about; *intensity* is. Activities such as hang gliding and snowboarding don't have "winners" or "losers." All are completely captivating. If the game isn't 100 percent engaging, their devotees want to know, why play at all? Did I succeed while playing? Did I fail? Who cares? What's your point?

History's real elite has always considered the distinction between winning and losing essentially beside the point. When confronting triumph or disaster, said Rudyard Kipling, they "treat these two impostors just the same." During discussions with CEOs of thriving companies, the terms success and failure rarely come up. Those who are fully engaged in life and consumed by what they're doing seldom stop to consider whether they're headed toward a win or a loss. Pursuing victory and avoiding defeat is not what the highest achievers are about. They're hunting for far bigger game.

2 · The Agony of Victory, the Thrill of Defeat

Long after he ended his career as one of basketball's all-time best players, Bill Russell made a startling admission: He found some games so absorbing and so intense that it made no difference to him who won or lost. This usually happened when his Boston Celtics played a team that was challenging them for the NBA championship. Three or four players on the floor would get hot. Their heat would spread to others. Then the whole game would—as Russell put it—"levitate." At this level of intensity, Russell only wanted the magic to continue. He wanted great plays to be made, regardless of who made them—even members of the other team. Russell's feelings went beyond joy to an exalted stratosphere in which lightning bolts of excitement raced up and down his spine. "On the five or ten occasions when the game ended at that special level," recalled the Celtics' star center in *Second Wind,* "I *literally* did not care who had won. If we had lost, I'd still be as free and as high as a sky hawk."

We assume that success is the pinnacle, failure the pits. They're not. The real pinnacle is when we are so engaged in what we're doing that this distinction vanishes. Athletes call it being *in the zone.* It isn't just athletes, of course. Any one of us can get so completely involved in some activity that we forget

13

about everything else. In a study of rock climbers, surgeons, chess players, factory workers, and dancers, psychologist Mihalyi Csikszentmihalyi found that when faced with extreme challenges they entered a state of elevated concentration—one he called *flow*—in which time seemed to stand still, one moment blended into the next, and doing the right thing became almost effortless. When completely consumed by an absorbing task they were oblivious to whether it "succeeded" or "failed."

Like Making Love

We've all had experiences like that. They could involve sailing a boat, building a cabinet, acting in a play, or developing a software program or a business plan. On the rare occasions when we achieve such a high level of intensity, we realize that peak experiences go beyond positive and negative, good and bad, victory and defeat. Like making love, our most engaging activities have nothing to do with winning and losing. They're a category unto themselves.

In any activity that's fully absorbing, the outcome is beside the point. Those who court triumph and risk catastrophe know this better than anyone. Their goal in life is not to succeed, make money, be happy, or be anything other than *engaged*. They enjoy a life rich with intensity and exhilaration. To genuine risk takers, the contrast between triumph and tragedy isn't as clear as it is to their more prudent brethren. They understand that both are *vivid* experiences. Each arouses strong, passionate feelings. They're allies in the struggle against mediocrity. Those who take bold chances don't think failure is the opposite of success. They believe that complacency is. Success and failure are both products of action, creativity, passion, energy, daring, courage, challenge. As biographer Tom Crouch observed of the Wright brothers, "They were as excited about failure as they were by success."

During dinner one evening in Dayton, Ohio, Wilbur Wright and renowned scientist Vannevar Bush compared notes on projects that hadn't gone anywhere. Wright then took Bush to his attic, where he showed him models of various odd gadgets. All were failed inventions of his. "I had plenty of similar efforts to tell him about," said Bush, "and we enjoyed ourselves thoroughly. Neither of us would have thus spilled things except to a fellow practitioner, one who had enjoyed the elation of creation and who knew that such elation is, to a true devotee, independent of practical results. So it is also, I understand, with poets."

Peak Experiences

Our most intense experiences exist in a universe beyond the usual labels of *good* or *bad*. At peak levels of intensity, emotions we consider positive or negative are hard to tell apart. Tears of joy differ little from ones of grief. The moans of a couple making love resemble those of wounded soldiers. Both pain and pleasure are aroused in the same center of our brains. The body itself can't distinguish strong feelings of any kind—anger, love, fear, excitement—until the mind tells it which is which. As Bill Russell and every other athlete discovers, memories of wins and losses grow vague. Moments of intensity remain vivid.

Think back to your adolescence. Some call this period the

best years of our lives. If *best* means *happiest,* that's true for very few. How many teenagers are happy? Most are too moody and self-absorbed. What our high school days are is *intense*—the most intense ones we may ever experience. That experience, like most memorable experiences, is too rich for simple labels like *good* or *bad.* Its intensity strikes deeper chords.

Those who achieve at a high level consider victory a poor substitute for exalted effort. In a winning-is-the-only-thing society like our own they seldom admit this. (Bill Russell said that, in his playing days, he would not have *dared* tell teammates that some games were so captivating he didn't care who won.) The irony is that some of history's biggest achievers—our most famous winners—didn't care a fig who won an activity they engaged in for its own sake.

More players and coaches agree with Bill Russell than say so out loud. Of course they would rather win. Who wouldn't? But that's not why they play the game. Win or lose, participating in athletic contests takes them to levels of passion enjoyed by few. That level grows out of striving to win, but it's every bit as dependent on the danger of loss. Victory and defeat both arouse strong feelings. Losing can be an even more intense experience than winning.

Craving Excitement

Those who study gamblers are usually surprised to discover how indifferent they are to loss. Gamblers themselves are fond of saying that the next best thing to winning is losing. Some even think there's more to be said for the latter. Losing demands more valor, more character, they say. As tragedy is to comedy, observed the late actor-gambler Walter Matthau, so does losing compare to winning. . . . "[B]igger, larger, stronger. Therefore more interesting."

Winning or losing is not the real goal of placing bets. Nor is making money. *Action* is the actual point of the exercise. *Excitement.* Being engaged in an activity that consumes 100 percent of your attention. Win or lose, having money riding on the outcome of an event is an intense experience. Like athletes, gamblers get in the zone. That's the main attraction of placing a bet. Money is an essential part of the exercise, because it creates the stakes that make gambling so exhilarating. Money is the means, however, not the end. Excitement is the end. To confirmed gamblers, winning is better than losing only because it means they get to play longer. This is why so many winners don't cash in their chips while they're ahead. To them that's the real loss. They're out of the action.

Risk takers of all kinds think in these terms. After dropping out of the Republican presidential primaries in 2000, Senator John McCain discovered that, even more than losing, he hated having to leave the hullabaloo of campaigning. "I really miss the excitement," McCain said later. For high-stakes political rollers, excitement is the thing, as it is with adventurers of every stripe. The tales they tell—of climbing crumbling rock faces, of steering kayaks swamped in rapids, of starting businesses that nearly collapsed—might make you wonder if the prospect of failure thrills them even more than the promise of success. You would be right to wonder. The risk of failure is far more captivating than success in the bag. That's why finding tragedy more engaging than triumph is not as irrational as it might sound. Any adventurer knows (but seldom admits) that the payoff for braving danger is not pleasure. Pleasure may even become boring.

Repeated too often, pleasurable experiences of all kinds grow predictable and, therefore, not pleasurable. Positive feelings lose their power to engage us faster than negative ones do. They routinely morph into monotony. To an excitement-craving person, monotony is more painful than misery.

Entrepreneurs are renowned for their excitement-craving temperaments. If anything, they prefer the dark clouds and thunderclaps of impending catastrophe to clear days of smoothly humming businesses. Research on entrepreneurial attitudes suggests that orderly settings cause these risk takers more pain than chaotic ones. "We have days when it's kind of smooth," the owner of a food-manufacturing business told *Inc.* magazine, "but those are not my greatest days." The founder of a restaurant chain concurred. "My eyes light up when I hear of a crisis," he said.

It's well recognized in psychology that some of us thrive in the midst of chaos but lose focus when things are going smoothly. For instance, before September 11, 2001, Rudy Giuliani was a controversial mayor of New York with an uneven record of achievement. Many considered him a divisive leader. During and after the collapse of the World Trade Center towers, however, New York's mayor was widely applauded for his masterful crisis management. The demands of dealing with calamity tapped resources of leadership Giuliani had never previously displayed. Individuals like him, who thrive in crisis, are well represented in the ranks of police officers, criminals, firefighters, paramedics, test pilots, business founders, and commodities traders. Such risk seekers don't just cope well with stress, they crave it.

Crisis Lovers

Those who are motivated more by the thrill of danger than the security of income can be found throughout the workplace. Some are entrepreneurs-to-be just waiting to escape. Others are *intrapreneurs,* who innovate and take chances within corporate ranks. Whatever they're called, every organization has employees who prefer the thrill of adversity to the tedium of triumph. The runup to success excites them. Success itself bores them. As Atari founder Nolan Bushnell discovered, "Being successful is kind of dull."

Excitement seekers like Bushnell would rather fail in thrilling fashion than succeed tediously. After the first flush of victory, success does get tedious. The philosopher Bertrand Russell once observed that success left one susceptible to boredom. Managers have to accommodate employees who find success boring by finding ways to keep their action level up. A new problem in need of solution is more arousing to them than one that's already solved.

To some extent this is true of everyone. Our spirits need regular stimulation as much as our bodies and minds do. Even as our rational brain says *avoid problems,* our nervous system begs to differ. *More complications,* it pleads. *Please! No problems mean no challenges, too little stimulation. I want to be more aroused, not less!* That's why our life can feel more meaningful when things are not going well than when they are. When our life is in disarray, we have challenging dilemmas to confront, exciting issues to discuss, greater sympathy for the problems of others. It's no surprise to psychologists that many people court adversity for the thrill and heroism of feeling on the edge.

Ask any founder of a thriving business how things are going and you'll get an aggravated recounting of payrolls to be met, debt to be serviced, insurance to be bought, and the need to expand. Running the business is a million headaches. Ask that person what it was like to *start* an enterprise, however, and watch his or her face light up. Getting a business off the ground is the heroic phase. Now, it's one thrilling story after another of bill collectors pounding on the door, creditors whistling through the keyholes, and eating peanut butter sandwiches on the floor by candlelight because the furniture was repossessed and electricity turned off. Those were the good old days when entrepreneurs won their stripes. Color comes to their faces as they recount such stories, and excitement rings in their voices.

It is a management truism that those who steer new businesses through storms of start-up adversity can't be trusted to run them once the sun comes out. Entrepreneurs typically are much better at *creating* enterprises than *managing* them. Their crisis-loving natures suit them better to the demands of impending catastrophe than to those of consolidating victory. Steadier management skills are now called for. Winning the gamble of starting a business means they're no longer buccaneers, explorers, wirewalkers. Now they're executives. For boredom-phobic entrepreneurs, this is not a welcome prospect. Even Nike's Phil Knight—who did a better job than most at making the transition from start-up rebel to responsible CEO—freely admitted that he found running a big company far less rewarding than starting a small one.

Today's entrepreneurs would have been yesterday's explorers, scouts, and warriors. The evolution of society has depended on their adventurous spirit. Nature has tried to tell us over the millennia that progress can be made only when failure is risked. This could be why we find adversity so alluring.

Sweet Adversity

Psychologist William James was unlucky enough to be in San Francisco during the 1906 earthquake. Its tremors threw him face down on the floor of his hotel room. The entire room trembled so violently that James felt as though he was in the mouth of a giant terrier shaking him like a rat. Furniture fell and slid around him. Wall plaster crumbled, filling the air with dust. A terrible roar assaulted his ears. The earthquake lasted for less than a minute (forty-eight seconds, according to the Lick Observatory). Surely William James looked back on that experience as one of unrelieved horror. Not at all. As the psychologist later wrote, his reaction to San Francisco's earthquake "consisted wholly of glee . . . I felt no trace whatever of fear, it was pure delight and welcome."

Here's a paradox: We typically avoid danger and seek security, yet remember most vividly—even fondly—those moments when we felt in peril. We push off from shore for what we hope will be a smooth sail toward a calm port. Afterward, we recall with greatest excitement and in sharpest detail the squalls that nearly swamped our boat. Memory is like that. Most of us have little trouble remembering what we were doing at the moment we heard that the World Trade Center towers were being attacked on September 11, 2001. Few can recall anything they did on September 10.

Adversity engraves deep memories. When looking back on a vacation, we're less likely to remember snapshot moments and more likely to recall ones of trial and tribulation. ("Do you remember the time when our tent collapsed in the rain and ... ?") Could our memories be telling us something? What they may be telling us is that human beings respond better to adversity—the danger of loss—than tranquillity. If we're too failure averse, we may never find that out. Nature would rather we did. A taste for affliction seems to be hardwired into our nervous systems. Certainly human beings have survived more bad times than good ones over the millennia. Perhaps that's why we've evolved to feel more alive during times of crisis than periods of calm. Our nervous systems are designed not just to endure but to flourish in the midst of calamity. This is as true in cubicles as in caves. Turning a crisis into a challenge that might eventually be rewarding is one of the most valuable of all management activities.

We keep having to rediscover not only how capable human beings are of coping with misfortune, but how well they rise to its challenges. When London was bombed during World War II, there was widespread concern that the psychological problems of Londoners would be severe. Just the opposite proved true. Admissions to mental hospitals dropped, as did the rate of suicide. By now, it's well established that during periods of war or civil unrest affected populations enjoy *reduced* rates of physical and mental illness. In the midst of Northern Ireland's extended strife, a notable decline in depressive illness, suicides, and cases of child abuse were recorded. During the turmoil and war of the 1960s and 1970s, student suicides dropped dramatically in the United States. Afterward, they rose again.

When asked what experiences most shaped their lives, people invariably mention some time of trial: the Depression, a business reverse, or near-fatal illness. Those who survive a brush with death typically say it was both the best and worst thing that ever happened to them. Worst, because it nearly killed them. Best, because it forced them to live life more fully, with a better sense of priorities.

Moments of crisis make us peer deeply within ourselves to see what's there. Generally, we're surprised by how much we find. We are all more rugged than we realize. We usually survive even devastating catastrophes in fine form. Studies have found that—within reason—coping with natural disasters can even enhance our psychological well-being. A study of Buffalo residents, twelve months after that city's worst blizzard in a century, found that those interviewed looked back on the sense of crisis and danger "almost nostalgically." Why shouldn't they? Such minidisasters force a break in routine, make us drop what we're doing, and focus full attention on exciting news. Parents become heroes to their children. Teenagers are faced with real—not contrived—challenges. One veteran of harrowing floods in Indiana later observed that those trying to hold back the rising waters included hundreds of students whom he had written off as irresponsible slackers. Now they worked the sandbag lines, hauled rubble, and helped evacuate the elderly. "Some were even ready to risk their lives if necessary," this man said. "And were they having a great time? The best ever."

Many Americans were surprised by the feelings of purpose, patriotism, and unity they experienced after the World Trade Center and Pentagon were attacked. This should not have been surprising. In the midst of adversity, we become our better selves. Neighbors who barely know each other work shoulder to shoulder. A sense of community emerges. As any combat veteran knows, we huddle together most closely when we're scared. During times of trial we crave the company of those in the same leaky boat. That's the success secret of support groups. It's also one reason why so many management training programs have become so daredevilish, sending participants hurtling through rapids, climbing up rock faces, and rappelling down cliffs. Ostensibly, these exercises help participants learn to manage stress. The bigger payoff is team building. Those who paddle through whitewater together stay close. Shared adversity is powerful glue.

Management by Calamity

When former Monsanto CEO Richard Mahoney asked employees what their *best* experience had been at work, most referred to some emergency. As difficulties mounted—flood waters destroyed seed stocks, or impossible demands were made by customers threatening to cancel a big order—everyone set aside their usual ways of doing things, ignored the clock, and pitched in to save the day. Afterward, like survivors of a battle, they swapped stories about individual acts of heroism. "Whether or not they win or lose," Mahoney's successor, Robert Shapiro, later noted in *The Soul at Work*, "whether the flood wins or they win, is less important than that they had this peak experience."

Crises can benefit individuals and organizations alike. They confront us with the paradox that human beings, alone or assembled, grow most from the situations they try hardest to avoid. Without the goad of impending catastrophe, we're too likely to just keep repeating what's worked in the past. The calamitous presidential election of 2000 forced Americans to confront vote-tabulation problems that should have been remedied decades earlier. Sometimes that's what it takes to blast through our lethargy and move us in needed new directions. The danger of failure forces us to revise our outlooks, open up, and take more chances.

As with individuals, sometimes crisis is the only thing that can move organizations. Like those who survive adversity and are better for it, organizations that struggle can develop a sense of cohesion and flexibility, and can find new ways of coping that keep them afloat when others sink. Paradoxically, adversity and upheaval can be far more powerful agents of change than planning and consultants. Without such goads, our resistance to needed innovation is usually too ingrained. The lesson for managers, obviously, is not to arrange calamities, but to recognize that calamities, when they do occur, can be opportunities for significant and needed change.

In organizational life, even the most tense, traumatic crises seldom damage the individuals involved. We are stronger than we think. So are those we work with. While organizations and relationships may be fragile, individuals are strong. The danger of crises is not so much to the individuals involved as to the organization of which they're a part, the complex set of often frail relationships that make up their social system. Management's main task in moments of crisis is to hold the organization together when it could easily fly apart. Managers remain composed while others are rattled. They keep larger goals in front of the group, adopt an optimistic posture toward the future, maintain a sense of humor, and take bold measures in response to developing events. These are not skills, but natural qualities, what we often call maturity. Sometimes a crisis calls upon us to reach deeply inside ourselves to find resources with which to meet it. Everyone has such resources. It can take a calamity to bring them out.

Even though individuals routinely acknowledge how important setbacks have been for their growth and development, managers seldom cite calamity as a catalyst for organizational change. Calamities embarrass them. They're likely to attribute any achievement that emerges from an organizational crisis to their management of it. That's often the case. However, there is also something to be said for the beneficial effects of plain old calamity. Without it, organizations would not be as strong, nor individuals as resourceful.

If adversity, crises, and the danger of failure are goads to progress, let's now examine the case that some have begun to make for the value of failure itself. The case for success is easy to make, and often made. The case for failure is far less obvious, but no less credible. It is neither masochistic nor irrational. Failure can even be a precondition of success.

3 · Nothing Succeeds Like Failure

Failure is one of the most emotionally loaded words in our language. It's among the experiences we try most to avoid. Understandably so. Sinking, sickening feelings accompany nearly any significant failure. We all know how painful, even crippling, these experiences can be, with their overwhelming, stomach-wrenching sense of loss.

The experience of failure can't be whitewashed. Nonetheless, the word itself can be redefined and the experience reassessed. Rather than cripple, failure can strengthen. Depending on how we respond to them, blows can shatter us as if we were a cheap clay pot or temper us as they would steel. Setbacks can even be antecedents to success. Managers can do much to convert an employee's sense of failure into one of experimentation, learning, and growth. By not labeling a plan, a design, or a product that doesn't work "a failure," we have the power to redefine that word.

Silicon Valley entrepreneurs already have. They consider failures to be rites of passage. "Learning experiences," such business creators call them, and "steps on the road to success." If you haven't failed, they say, you're not trying hard enough. It's a truism in Silicon Valley that a high tolerance for failure underlies this sector's dynamism. There, one is told repeatedly, "We tolerate failure here." One of the main ways in which Valleyites see themselves as a breed apart is in their acceptance of business reverses as normal. The essence of that attitude is a conviction that setbacks aren't necessarily a backward step. Paul Saffo, director of the Institute for the Future in nearby Menlo Park, compared the Valley's many failed enterprises to fires in a forest that clear space for new growth. Business failures, Saffo told *The New York Times,* are "an important part of our ecosystem."

Not only is there little stigma attached to going bankrupt among cutting-edge entrepreneurs, it's even seen as a good source of business experience. Some job recruiters prefer bankrupted start-up founders to corporate executives who never failed because they never took a chance. Far from shunning start-uppers who have lost their gambles, venture capitalists in Silicon Valley court them as once burned, twice wise. "I like a situation where I can benefit from the mistakes a guy's made with someone else's money," explained one. Many sober investors agree. They look to Silicon Valley as a harbinger, the place where trends begin—not just because of the technological prowess of its engineers but because of the boldness of its entrepreneurs.

The failure-tolerant Silicon Valley mindset is seeping into the rest of the country's economy, and the world's. It suggests an important shift in our thinking which is not merely generational, geographical, or the latest management fad. It's neither *new economy* nor *old economy.* This change of attitude has a clear basis in psychological research. There are sound management reasons for being more accepting of failure and less impressed by success.

That is not an altogether modern insight. In fact, a failure-friendly attitude characterized America's leading inventor-moguls as far back as Thomas Edison, the Wright brothers,

Henry Ford, and Thomas J. Watson. No one, however, embraced failure with greater passion than Charles Kettering.

Bards of Failure

When he died in 1958, Charles Kettering was considered second only to Thomas Edison as America's leading inventor-mogul. Kettering's two hundred patents included one for the electric self-starter that revolutionized car engines. He also played a major role in developing refrigerants, antiknock gasoline, diesel engines, quick-drying auto paint, and home air conditioners. These innovations made Kettering a wealthy man, as the founder of Delco and a long-time General Motors vice president.

One key to Kettering's success was his poor eyesight. Kettering's eyes were so easily strained that college classmates had to read his textbooks aloud to him. He dropped out of Ohio State more than once due to severe eyestrain. Later, as an engineer, Kettering had difficulty reading the blueprints, spec sheets, and statistics of his trade. This problem forced him to rely on his own inner vision. In the process he saw a bigger, richer, more interesting picture.

Perhaps due to his own experience, Kettering had little time for conventional education. He thought that genuine innovators were hobbled more than helped by what they had learned in school. Overly educated people were the ones least likely to make new discoveries, Kettering contended, because they were too intent on doing things the way they had been taught. He felt that students subjected to the prospect of failing exams and "flunking out" learned a bad lesson: that failure is terminal. For Kettering, it was the other way around. A good research man, he liked to say, failed every time but the last one. If he failed 999 times and succeeded on the thousandth, the last effort was the only one that mattered. "He treats his failures as practice shots," said Kettering. "Boss Ket" told younger colleagues that he himself had been wrong 99.9 percent of the time. What every educated person needed to learn, Kettering felt, was that "it is not a disgrace to fail, and that he must analyze each failure to find its cause . . . [he] must learn how to fail intelligently. Failing is one of the greatest arts in the world. One fails toward success."

The attitudes of today's entrepreneurs differ little from those of yesterday's inventor-moguls. Henry Ford called failure "the opportunity to begin again, more intelligently." He spoke from experience. Before the Ford Motor Company succeeded, two previous ventures of his had failed. Like contemporary innovators, earlier pathbreakers disdained "success" on conventional terms and saw much to be said for setbacks. "The fastest way to succeed" said IBM head Thomas Watson, Sr., in his younger years, "is to double your failure rate."

A philosophical attitude toward failure characterizes business founders everywhere. They tend to regard the prospect of going belly up as the price of progress. Most of them endure multiple setbacks before a venture succeeds. A study of forty successful entrepreneurs found that most had run one or more businesses into the ground. Yet the vast majority said if their current venture collapsed, they would start another. *Don't they ever learn?* the more prudent among us wonder. Well, no. That's why entrepreneurs keep plugging. Getting knocked down. Trying again. On the floor. Back on their feet. Like wirewalkers, venture founders know that whoever gets on the wire may fall off, they just don't consider this sufficient reason to stay on the ground.

Last century's inventors, yesterday's entrepreneurs, and to-day's start-uppers share an adventurous temperament. They resemble explorers more than executives, even in their management style. Such swashbucklers subscribe to the philosophy that experiments can't fail, and imbue the organizations they create with that philosophy. A reluctance to try something new, they say, is worse than trying something new that fails. Among them, there's almost a cult of failure, a cocky pride in their ability to take a hit and come back swinging. If anything, they revel in their setbacks, seeming almost to brag about how many times they've had to get up off the mat. Some feel that they can't fully assess another person until he or she has been tested by adversity. Coca-Cola's late chief Roberto Goizueta said he only trusted those managers whom he had seen make a significant strategic error. High achievers of all kinds are more impressed by spectacular defeats than modest victories. Such achievers don't love to lose. They are not perverse or masochistic. Rather, they understand that big failure is usually a product of high aspiration. "In great attempts," said Vince Lombardi, "it is glorious even to fail."

Splendid Failure

Of all his novels, William Faulkner liked *The Sound and the Fury* best. Why? Because the Nobel Prize–winning author considered it his biggest failure. "All of us have failed to reach our dream of perfection," Faulkner explained of himself and his fellow writers. "So I rate us on the basis of our splendid failure to do the impossible."

Faulkner's attitude typifies risk takers. Bold visionaries of all kinds have the highest regard for failure. In their minds, failure implies you've taken a chance. The bigger the failure, the bigger the chance you took. A huge failure suggests you've overreached—tried for something grand—rather than settled for a small success. "A man's life is interesting primarily when he has failed—I well know," said the French statesman Georges Clemenceau. "For it's a sign that he tried to surpass himself."

This attitude is hard to appreciate in our *Just win, baby* society. While failure can be due to incompetence, poor judgment, or circumstances beyond our control, it may simply mean that we took a risk and lost. That's the nature of risk taking. Genuine risk takers anticipate failure. "I think if you don't fail a certain percent of the time," said writer-director Michael Crichton, "it means you're playing it too safe."

The essence of risk is failure. Daring leads to loss more often than gain. Baseball players admire an infielder who makes extra errors lunging for out-of-reach balls more than one who makes fewer errors because he sticks to high-percentage plays. In pursuits of all kinds, apparent success is too often a result of keeping one's aspirations low. Big wins are enjoyed only by those who risk huge losses. "I've missed more than nine thousand shots in my career," admitted Michael Jordan. "I've lost almost three hundred games. Twenty-six times I've been trusted to take the winning shot and missed. I've failed over and over and over again in my life. And that is why I succeed."

We hear often about the triumphs of those the world considers "success stories." What we seldom hear about are the many setbacks that preceded their victories—and contributed to them. Like the careers of so many top executives, that of AOL Time-Warner's Gerald Levin was littered with flops. They included *TV-Cable Week,* the information service Teletext, and the costly Full Service Network, in Orlando, Florida. These unsuccessful ventures cost Levin's company hundreds of millions of dollars. His triumphs, however, earned Time-Warner far more. In speeches, Time-Warner's CEO cited H. G. Wells's fanciful game *Cheat the Prophet* to explain his approach. In this game, one gathers the sharpest, most perceptive group of futurists available, asks them to forecast coming events, then pursues projects they consider too preposterous to consider. From this pool of ideas will come resounding successes—and major mistakes.

Productive Mistake Making

While part of the research and development team at Apple, David Levy was reprimanded by his boss for not making enough mistakes. Levy's boss said he wanted no less than 80 percent failure in ventures he attempted. Only then would he know that Levy was actually trying anything new. Levy took the advice to heart. Now a freelance inventor, he lives by the credo that "If I'm not failing enough, I'm not doing my job."

To the true innovator, there's no such thing as a mistake. Each miscue is considered part of the process, a marker on the map that says where not to go. Such markers are every bit as important as those that point in the right direction, if not more so. To inventors, it's not even clear what's actually a miscue.

Trying to minimize or avoid slipups could have stifled some awfully important innovations. So-called accidents have been wholly or partly responsible for products such as Gore-Tex, Nylon, Teflon, Silly Putty, penicillin, shatterproof glass, and the microwave oven.

The world belongs to those who don't let anxiety about screwing up keep them from moving forward. Those who are too afraid to make a mistake work for those who aren't. Even harder than making our own mistakes is letting others make theirs. When a manager sees an employee setting off on the wrong path, the natural temptation is to jump in and say, "Wait. Let me show you what to do." Fighting that temptation may cause problems in the short run, but lead to new discoveries in the long run. At 3M they say, "The captain bites his lip until it bleeds," meaning that, once managers put their money on a project, they back off. This reduces errorphobia among innovators and allows them to pursue their own productive mistake making.

Among ninety managers he interviewed while doing research on leadership, Warren Bennis found that the most effective ones not only didn't shy away from ventures that might fail, but actively sought them out. When their efforts went south, they considered this a valuable form of education. "If I have an art form of leadership," one told Bennis, "it is to make as many mistakes as quickly as I can in order to learn."

Like better managers, artists themselves tend to be philosophical about mistakes. Some consider slipups invaluable deviations from their norm that can enhance, not diminish, a painting, sculpture, or piece of music. The Beatles routinely incorporated studio mishaps into their recordings, including the memorable opening to "I Feel Fine," which was a product of unintended feedback when John Lennon leaned his acoustic guitar on an amplifier and Paul McCartney plucked a string on his electric bass. In years to come, mistakes in certain products will become status symbols. As production techniques and computer imaging make flawless arts and crafts commonplace, minor flaws will constitute evidence that one's rug or ceramic mug is one of a kind, at least until computers are programmed to generate flaws randomly.

Artists, inventors, and product developers aren't the only ones who recognize the value of mistakes. Basketball coach Ward "Piggy" Lambert used to tell his players "The team that makes the most mistakes will probably win." What's that you say? Don't sportscasters routinely introduce games with just the opposite statement? And who's Piggy Lambert? His name may have faded into the mists of athletic history, but one of Lambert's players at Purdue—John Wooden—went on to achieve coaching immortality. Like Lambert, Wooden preached the gospel of productive mistake making. "The *doer* makes mistakes," he said. " . . . mistakes come from doing, but so does success."

Imperfections are the essence of evolution. Success as a species depends on mistakes. Design errors lead to mutations that produce traits better suited to survival. Continued progress depends on new flaws appearing. Some species adapt so well to a single niche that design flaws no longer help them evolve. They do fine just as they are in an undemanding environment. Enjoying success in too narrow an environment can lead to extinction, however. Many endangered species can survive only in a very limited ecosystem.

The same thing is true of organizations. Those that do well in too small a pond grow increasingly limited in their vision. They get set in their ways. They don't benefit from their mistakes and see no need to do so. Reinforcement for doing things a certain way makes them errorphobic and change resistant. Then they can seek protection (i.e., subsidies) or become extinct (i.e., bankrupt). Such organizations might have been better off if they had migrated to a big lake where they were forced to make more mistakes—global markets, say—and evolved to meet that challenge.

Like living organisms, companies that don't make mistakes adapt poorly to changing conditions. Any group that includes too many members paralyzed by a fear of stumbling is one preparing for its own demise. The larger and more bureaucratized they become, the more likely this is to be true. Intolerance of errors is the Achilles' heel of too-mature corporations.

Even though failure is always a possible result when new things are tried, that isn't necessarily a bad thing. Economists consider a high rate of business failure a sign of economic vitality. A rising rate of bankruptcies means that more businesses than ever are being started. One secret of America's economic health is that bankruptcy carries so little stigma. In American society, one gets many chances, and financiers recognize that early failures can be used as stepping stones to later success. This acceptance of business failure as normal, even desirable, is at the heart of our economy's dynamic growth.

Continued success requires regular setbacks, even spectacular blunders. After all, Coca-Cola's fabled CEO Roberto Goizueta sponsored one of the most catastrophic blunders in American business history: the introduction of New Coke. New Coke was such a world-class gaffe that it's second only to the Edsel in the annals of marketplace bloopers. But what better way to convey the idea that big new ideas are in order, win or lose? Goizueta's reputation as a visionary risk taker was actually enhanced by the black eye he suffered from backing New Coke. Furthermore, it took this calamity—in which, favorable taste tests notwithstanding, customers were enraged by having *their* Coke pulled from the market—to make Goizueta realize that the real value of Coca-Cola lay not in its formula, but in its brand.

It may not seem that way to those who have failed, but managers in the United States are far less stigmatized by failure than their counterparts are abroad. Failure tolerance is the essence of the entrepreneurial boldness that has prepared America so well for a rapidly changing economy. This attitude attracts entrepreneurs from around the world who crave the opportunity to risk failure. One burden older economies have had to bear is their intolerance of failure. In societies many Americans' ancestors fled, going broke can be a disastrous humiliation. A businessman in Germany said that "panic" was the most common reaction in his sector to any type of failure. That attitude makes the stakes of embarking on a venture catastrophically high. "There is not a positive attitude toward risk taking," agreed a French computer company executive about his own culture "If you take a risk and fail, you are finished."

Risk is a taboo concept in failurephobic cultures. Too many in such settings see only its downside: an opportunity to lose money, time, and face. The problem in conservative economies is not one of technology shortfall, what's in short supply is a willingness to risk making a mistake.

One reason for the collapse of the Soviet Union was that its state-controlled economy grew obsessively intolerant of mistakes. Employees in Soviet workplaces were terrified to try anything new. They left that sort of thing to capitalist entrepreneurs. The downfall of the Soviet economy was due in part to its inability to accommodate failure. Socialism in its Stalinist garb was so failurephobic that Soviet companies were propped up, subsidized, and allowed to stumble along for decades after they had actually failed.

The essence of a free-market economy is constant correction based on continual consumer feedback in response to errors. For corrections to occur, mistakes must be made. More mistakes being made usually means more experiments are being tried. A rising level of errors can be evidence that an innovative climate is emerging. This casts failure in a whole new light. It could mean an organization is beginning to change in important and necessary ways. What at first looks like a setback could be just the opposite: a harbinger of impending success.

Success Disguised as Failure

In psychotherapy, patients making progress continue to show discontent, but about healthier concerns. Their complaints may change from, "I'm depressed" to "I'm not living up to my potential." They reach a level of higher-order discontent.

That's true in the workplace, too. Managers often feel they've failed when their actions produce complaints and demands. However, the paradox of rising expectations (i.e., revolutions are more likely as social conditions improve than when they're hopeless) suggests that when things get better, employee grumbling persists—and may even get louder—but about a higher level of concern. When this happens, managers can take the same approach therapists do, and see complaints as evidence of progress, not problems. It's not achieving contentment that matters, but improving the quality of discontent.

Progress seldom leads to serenity, nor should it. A serene work force is unlikely to try new things. Creative workers gripe a lot, but at a high level. They don't complain about cafeteria food or vacation schedules. They're concerned about having the leeway and support to create something new. They want their talents to be utilized. They crave a challenge. Whether those challenges lead to so-called success or what others call failure doesn't concern them

We hear often about "costly failures." Complacency costs more. Failures inch us forward, making it possible for others to take great strides in our wake. The corollary, of course, is that success can be dangerous. This sounds preposterous. It's not. Success can take a terrible toll on individuals and organizations alike. If failure has a surprising upside, success has an equally surprising downside.

4 · Nothing Fails Like Success

A condition has been identified that characterizes many who get rich quickly: *sudden wealth syndrome*. As with any major life change, the unexpected change of status among those who make overnight killings forces stressful adaptations. Friends don't necessarily appreciate their success. Casual conversations about kids, cars, and clogged gutters are no longer possible. ("How would *you* know?") The suddenly wealthy, in turn, resent their friends' wariness. Yet once they've treated themselves to a new Mercedes, a bigger home, and a trip to Tahiti, they typically find themselves no happier than before. "In a lot of ways I was happier living a simpler life," one newly wealthy executive told the *Los Angeles Times*. "I'm not saying I'm a miserable guy, but it is hard talking to people about making this transition. Other people just think, 'Shut up! You have what everyone dreams of.' What they don't understand is that change is always difficult, and sometimes it's painful."

Since the challenges of failure are so much more obvious, painful, and universal, it's easy to scoff at the very notion that success might also be challenging. Sometimes, it takes a headline to call our attention to the fact that no matter how sweet, success has a sour side, too. It seems so inexplicable when those who apparently have it made stumble: enter rehab, shoplift, commit suicide. Obviously, they had more problems than we could see.

Why should success pose problems? The obvious explanation

is human perversity, an inability to enjoy one's blessings, a sense that we don't deserve to succeed. Such feelings are typically grouped under the heading *fear of success*. That much-studied syndrome is usually treated as a problem to solve, a disease in need of cure, a product of self-contempt. The stress of success, however, seldom has anything to do with self-contempt or any other kind of neurosis. There are compelling, rational reasons to find success challenging—more challenging in some cases than failure.

Marooned by Success

Dustin Hoffman once said that if he had known how much success awaited him, he never would have become an actor. The Oscar-winning movie star explained that he began acting expecting to fail. He was mistaken, and sorry about it. Hoffman found that the costs of success included not only a serious loss of privacy, but having to forego the company of failed actors. The latter was especially frustrating. According to Hoffman, failed actors were much better company than successful ones. That's not true just of actors. In general, those who aren't successful (on the world's terms) tend to be better company than those who are. They not only have more sympathy for others, but more time to spend with them.

Success is extremely time consuming. Scheduling becomes a problem. ("I might be able to see you for a quick lunch next month.") Those who get to the top and want to stay there have little room on their calendars for much else: hobbies, travel, family, friends. A pal is someone you can call, or drop in on, at a moment's notice. This is seldom possible after one becomes prominent. Prominent people are understandably wary of those who want to be their friend, seeing among them lots of opportunists and sycophants. Relationships that once were casual now are scrutinized. What does this person want from me?

After one of two friends climbs a ladder, they approach each other differently from when both were on the ground looking up. Back then, they were at ease with each other. Even if their friendship continues, its ease disappears. Genuine friendship is best enjoyed by those on a par. The postsuccess alternative is to make new friends among fellow success stories. These new friendships are seldom as satisfying as the old ones, however. Those doing well on *People* magazine's terms rarely enjoy each other's company. "The penalty of success" said Lady Astor, "is to be bored by people who used to snub you."

Successful people are caught on the horns of a dilemma. Successes can no more pal around with nonsuccesses than generals can fraternize with privates. But in the world of the successful, pals on a par are potential rivals, therefore not really pals at all. The farther up the ladder one climbs, the less camaraderie one enjoys.

This flies in the face of conventional wisdom. Our assumption is that failures are shunned like lepers, while successful people are surrounded by admirers who adore their success and, hence, them. That's not how it is at all. According to Bette Midler, "The worst part of success is trying to find someone who is happy for you." When we're doing well and report that news to others, we would like to think they'll be happy for us, and that our success will make us more popular. This is seldom true.

"Anyone can sympathize with the sufferings of a friend," said Oscar Wilde, "but it requires a very fine nature to sympathize with a friend's success."

There's a German word—*schadenfreude*—that refers to the guilty pleasure of hearing about someone else's misfortune. There is no comparable word for the joy of hearing about another person's good fortune because that feeling is so rare. When someone else tells us how well they're doing, instead of feeling pleasure, we often feel rotten. That response—if we can allow ourselves to experience and identify such a seemingly insensitive reaction—typically leads to envy, followed by resentment, then anger, and despair. It is a normal, predictable, and widespread re-action, and is an integral part of the downside of success. Former Texas football coach Darrell Royal once observed that even his friends didn't like him to be *too* successful. Luckily, Royal added, he'd lost enough games over the years to maintain his friendships.

It is utterly human to respond better to travail than triumph. The setbacks of others remind us of our own. Everyone fails. Only a handful succeed. Since even apparently successful people rarely *feel* successful, however, a sense of failure is the most common human condition. Hearing about someone else's diffi-culties elicits our humanity. We empathize with those in distress and want to lend them a hand, or at least a sympathetic ear.

Early in his career, Lou Holtz was an assistant to Ohio State's legendary football coach Woody Hayes. When Holtz left OSU to become head coach at William & Mary, Hayes said to call him anytime. As he recounted in *Winning Every Day,* Holtz did, sometimes with problems, more often just to chat and report how well things were going. In time, Hayes stopped returning his calls. Finally an exasperated Holtz told Hayes's secretary that he had a problem and *needed* to talk with the coach. Hayes called him right back. Before getting to his problem, Holtz asked Hayes why he no longer returned his calls. Hayes responded, "You don't need me to tell you what a good job you're doing or how much the alums love you. You have enough people doing that. I'm returning *this* call because you have a problem and I'm here to help."

Everybody Hates a Winner

One of the least expected and most stressful results of success is the antipathy of others. It's simply not true that everybody loves a winner. Winners arouse admiration and envy, but little real affection. Our apparent love of winners is actually an infatuation that burns brightly during the spring of triumph, but fades quickly in the winter of decline. Plucky losers, on the other hand—Bob Uecker, Ralph Kramden, Charlie Chaplin's Little Tramp—inspire lasting devotion. Yankee fans come and go; the loyalty of Cub fans is legendary. Few remember who won medals during the 1984 Olympics, but who can forget the rubbery-legged Swiss marathoner Gabrielle Andersen-Scheiss staggering across the finish line in last place? We've heard often that adversity tells you who your friends are. Success does, too. Failure and success both reveal who really cares about us—the ones who stick with us through thin and thick. If anything, success identifies genuine friends more surely than failure does.

Successful people (on society's terms) routinely find friends from the past disappear. They usually explain this by saying such friends were envious. The old friends themselves say their former chum has changed, isn't the same good guy he used to be. He hasn't got time for them anymore. Both are right, and neither.

For those who are less prominent, the real issue is how a pal's success makes *them* feel. In a thoughtful essay on this subject, Thomas Powers pointed out that the rise of an old friend forces others to question whether they've become the person they set out to be. Few have. That's why nervous diffidence is the norm when those who haven't achieved their goals confront old friends who have. The drifting apart that follows is not drifting at all. It's more like a divorce. Even though this split is usually initiated by the less successful of the two, its motivation has more to do with self-doubt than hostility. "I do not think we mind so much what others do as what *we* have not done," Powers concluded, "that we are less envious of success than diminished by our own failure."

This is why, when a good friend embarks on a journey that might reach a lofty destination, we're likely to be ambivalent. As a friend, we want them to succeed, but another voice within prays that they won't. Gore Vidal once admitted that whenever a friend of his succeeded, "a little something in me dies." Vidal spoke for many. That sentiment is not as spiteful as it sounds. Sure, it's partly a product of jealousy. But there's more, too. We know it's unlikely that our friendship will survive a friend's triumph.

The Personal Price of Success

After winning an Academy Award, actress Julie Christie said she not only didn't deserve the gold statuette in her hands but was embarrassed by it. Christie had been advised to talk herself out of feeling this way. She couldn't. Despite her best efforts, long after winning an Oscar the actress told *Cosmopolitan* that she still regarded her success as "a sort of little mangy dog that's following you around, and you just can't get rid of it!"

Success on worldly terms is achieved with titles, salaries, awards, fame. Winning an Oscar. Appearing on *The Oprah Winfrey Show*. Being listed in *Who's Who*. The lucky few who succeed on these terms don't necessarily feel they've earned their laurels, however. Those whom the world considers successful are more circumspect about this status. Henry Thoreau thought success was "slow suicide." William James called it a "bitch-goddess." Graham Greene considered success little more than "delayed failure." As Emily Dickinson wrote,

> *Success is counted sweetest*
> *By those who ne'er succeed*

Those who win public recognition seldom feel like clean and clear winners. This is especially true of award winners, who usually realize how much politics are involved in the honor they have received. Awards can be bestowed or withheld for entirely arbitrary reasons. (Graham Greene never won a Nobel Prize in literature because *one* member of the nominating committee blackballed him every time his name was considered.) Behind most prizes, trophies, medals, and awards is a melodrama of politics, favoritism, favors, orthodoxy, fashion, intrigue, and hidden agendas. Some newspapers employ editors whose main assignment is to pursue Pulitzer Prizes. Discreet campaigns for Nobels are commonplace. Movie studios spend millions of dollars advertising their Oscar-nominated products on the accurate assumption that this will help them win. The tail wags the dog. Winning prizes becomes more important than doing work worthy of one. (Which is why the ad agency Wells, Rich, Green does not allow their creative people to apply for awards; it takes their focus off serving clients.) Small wonder that those who win honors on these terms wonder what they really signify—if anything.

History's assessment routinely conflicts with that of contemporary award givers. In 1929, the year Thomas Wolfe's *Look Homeward, Angel,* Ernest Hemingway's *A Farewell to Arms,* and William Faulkner's *The Sound and the Fury* were published, novelist Julia M. Peterkin won the Pulitzer for her now long-forgotten novel *Scarlet Sister Mary.* Those who win Nobels seldom produce anything of consequence thereafter. Oscar winners routinely end up in mediocre movies. Far from being motivated, any high achiever can be inhibited by such recognition: jinxed by a Nobel, become a Heisman Trophy benchwarmer, or get cut from a team after appearing on *Sports Illustrated*'s cover.

Success is at least as hazardous as failure. It means redefining our sense of self around being a success rather than an unfinished portrait. (This is a much tougher task than it sounds to those who have never had to try.) We also no longer have failure to blame for feeling unhappy. If success can't make us happy, we then must ask, what can? If we don't feel successful *and* our life is problematic, it's easy to see a connection. Obviously, we surmise, the reason we have so many problems is our lack of success. Having made that connection, the assumption follows that once we do enjoy some success, our problems will vanish. Even gold-plated faucets leak, however, fan belts in a Mercedes still need to be replaced, and headwaiters don't always acknowledge one's achievements with their restaurent's best table. Spouses pick postsuccess fights, teenagers remain sullen, spiritual voids stay empty.

According to Deion Sanders, fame and fortune simply bring out what's already inside in a person. In his case it was spiritual despair. The fabulously wealthy football star subtitled his memoir *How Success Nearly Ruined My Life.* In this book, Sanders explained that the more acclaim he won and the more money he made, the emptier he felt inside. Even after helping Dallas win the Super Bowl, Sanders simply packed his gear and fled the locker room.

Many imagine that possessing what Sanders had—fame, wealth, athletic ability—would make them ecstatic. It didn't do that for him. "It's not what you think it is," Deion said of the success he found so unrewarding, "I had that stuff and I was your basic human crash dummy." Those who succeed must be prepared to handle it. Sanders wasn't. Neither expensive cars, jewelry, elaborate parties, nor women in multiples lifted his spirits. As he later wrote, "When I achieved every goal I could think of, I was right back where I started. Empty, empty, empty, and nothing I did could touch that deep loneliness inside me."

Feeling Like a Fraud

One of the first things psychotherapists learn is that, regardless of appearances, *nobody has it made.* When success is accompanied by fame, achieving an inner sense of accomplishment can be that much more difficult. Winning too much recognition can make it harder, not easier, to develop the self-knowledge that is the essence of maturity. Instead, understandably, we would rather accept the world's verdict that we're fabulous. When questions arise about that verdict, we may lack the resources to cope. As *Time's* Karl Taro Greenfeld said of his friend Jay Moloney, the wunderkind Hollywood agent who represented top clients and made millions of dollars in his mid-twenties before becoming addicted to cocaine and committing suicide at thirty-five, "he never had a chance to figure out who he was, beneath all the trappings of worldly success."

Feeling genuinely successful requires reflection. The pursuit of recognition allows little time for that. It takes only a bit of thought to realize how little it all means. That's why, no matter how lionized they are by the public, few feel successful inside, the place where it matters most. Winning recognition for accomplishments we don't respect only magnifies a sense of being an impostor. Public acclaim adds little to an inner sense of worth, and can even make us feel fraudulent, as the gap between the outer and the inner grows. Just a moment's reflection raises questions about whether the achievements for which we've been rewarded have anything to do with the person we know ourselves to be. The higher our trajectory, the more susceptible we are to such sentiments. The more recognition we earn, the greater the gap grows between who we appear to be and who we actually are. As an old joke goes, if someone were to stand outside a hotel housing a CEO convention and yell, "Run! We've been found out!" the rooms would empty quickly.

In his book *Life and Work,* James Autry observed that we should never assume that those whom we admire, who seem to have achieved goals beyond our own range, are as happy, secure, self-assured, or fulfilled as we imagine. He offered himself as Exhibit A. While CEO of the Meredith Magazine Group, Autry had lunch with a friend who was a vice president of one of the country's largest companies. Midway through lunch, his friend asked abruptly, "Do you ever get the feeling that one day they are going to come into your office and say, 'Okay, Autry, we found out about you'?"

"Yes, yes," Autry replied without hesitating. He told his friend that he felt that way often. And him? The friend nodded. They both laughed.

"It's as if we're still the little boys playing with the big boys," Autry's friend said. "We don't really belong here, do we?"

"Of course not," agreed Autry. "In the big office with the big salary and the perks? Of course not. That's for the big boys."

"And do you know what this tells us?" the friend continued. "There are no big boys, only us little boys."

The two then discussed the self-doubts that made each feel that he really didn't belong in big-time business. In high school, neither had played football, been popular with girls, or owned a car. Both felt driven by wounds in their early lives to *prove* their worth with the trappings of success, trappings they weren't sure they deserved. And what about the kids who did play football, Autry and his friend wondered, the ones who did own their own cars and were popular with girls. What happened to them?

Looking Back on a Great Future

Those who attend high school reunions are often astonished to discover how undistinguished their biggest-deal classmates have become. Football stars read gas meters, cheerleaders check out groceries, valedictorians check out books, and most likely to succeeds are assistants to associate vice presidents.

Think back to your own high-school days. Who won the most acclaim? What are they doing now? Have any fulfilled their adolescent promise? If they have, they're exceptional. Studies of high-school graduates rarely find any correlation between recognition in high school and recognition thereafter. If anything, success during adolescence makes it harder, not easier, to succeed later on. The terms are too different. What worked in high school seldom works later on. Good looks, a winning smile, the right shoes, living on the best side of town, no longer count for much.

Those not tested by setbacks when young may never learn how to rebound from defeat. Too much success at an early age can build a fragile foundation. The confidence early success induces can be misleading in a postgraduate world that has higher standards for achievement. High expectations heaped on young success stories are more hobble than boost. Perhaps that is why high school's most likely to succeeds so often end up working for those who were more obscure—in some cases, their own classmates. Charlie Ross, who was valedictorian of his high school's senior class and editor of its newspaper later became press secretary for his classmate Harry Truman, who did little of note in high school. Mack McLarty, Mr. Everything in his Hope, Arkansas, high school (all-district quarterback, student council president, Boy's State Governor) later worked for his childhood friend Bill Clinton in the White House, until he got eased out. Clinton himself lost an election for secretary of his senior class at Hot Springs High School. His predecessor Franklin Roosevelt said he had felt "hopelessly out of things" as a student at Groton. FDR's biographer John Gunther observed that "The boys who were the best 'Grotties' usually turned out to be nonentities later; boys who hated Groton did much better."

Most schools do a remarkably poor job of recognizing and rewarding future achievers. Why should this be? There's a clear explanation. The standards for success in school have very little to do with standards thereafter. Their aptitude tests predict only an ability to get good grades. Studies rarely find any correlation between success in school (i.e., good grades) and success thereafter. In some cases, it's just the opposite. When Fred Smith wrote a paper at Yale outlining his vision for an overnight delivery service, Smith's professor said that although this plan was interesting, in order to receive better than a C, his idea had to be "feasible." That plan later became the basis for Federal Express. A few years later, twenty-one-year-old Yale architecture student Maya Ying Lin was given a B for her proposed Vietnam veterans memorial of polished black marble cutting a graceful swath into the ground. According to Lin, her professor didn't think this unorthodox approach was suited to a war memorial. Lin submitted her design to the veterans' committee anyway. It was chosen—unanimously—from among more than 1,500 entries. Today, Maya Lin's Vietnam Veterans Memorial is considered one of the most powerful monuments ever built. Lin herself has become one of the nation's leading architects.

In his career-long study of millionaires, Thomas Stanley has not only found no correlation between success in school and an ability to accumulate wealth, he's actually found a negative correlation. Few of Stanley's millionaires got good grades or high SAT scores. His wealthy subjects rarely showed up in any "most" category during high school (most talented, most popular, most likely to succeed). After graduating from college (seldom a prestigious one) their lack of sparkling academic records kept many from getting hired by top corporations. As a result, they were forced to start their own enterprises. In effect, they hired themselves.

"It seems that school-related evaluations are poor predictors of economic success," Stanley concluded in *The Millionaire Mind*. What did predict economic success was a willingness to take risks. By contrast, the success–failure standards of most schools penalized risk takers. As we've seen, in business, sports, science, and the arts there's a certain regard for gallant failure by those who take big chances. In school, however, an F is an F: bad news. You flunked. You're a failure.

Far from rewarding those who take chances, most educational systems honor those who play it safe. They're the ones who get good grades. As a result, those who do well in school find it hard to take risks later on. That's not what won them academic honors. The ones who do take chances have a hard time in school and are often penalized for their independent ways. Many of Stanley's subjects said teachers told them "You'll never succeed," or "That's the dumbest idea for a new business I have ever heard." Paradoxically, the seeds of their future success were planted in such messages. Withering criticism weeded out those who couldn't take the heat. The ones who could were able to use their critics as goads, doubters to prove wrong.

Goads push us harder than rewards. What are the A students from Fred Smith's class up to now? How about those whose memorial designs Maya Lin's professor liked better than hers?

And what ever happened to the basketball players who made the team at North Carolina's Laney High School the day Michael Jordan didn't? When the list of those who had made the varsity was posted during his sophomore year, Jordan's wasn't on it. He hurried home, threw himself on his bed, and wept bitter tears. Jordan then dedicated himself to proving that Clifton Herring—the coach who cut him—had made a mistake. This vow drove him to become perhaps the best basketball player ever. Those who did make Laney's team the day Michael Jordan didn't are today remembered only in yearbook pictures. "I never dreamed Michael would end up where he is today," Clifton Herring later marveled. "Michael just wasn't good enough." Then.

That's what makes assessing talent so difficult. As with mutual funds, when it comes to athletes—and people in general, past performance is no guarantee of future results. Those who succeed at one level don't necessarily excel at the next. Too many of them hit a plateau. They don't develop the will to keep progressing because it never seemed necessary. Being told once too often how good they were deprived them of the nemeses, the goads, the Clifton Herrings to *show* a thing or two. Athletes we hear about as adults typically have a long list of skeptics to prove wrong. Some of the biggest stars in professional sports—Kurt Warner, Terrell Davis, Mike Piazza—were low draft picks, or not picked at all. By contrast, "can't miss" minor league prospects routinely fail to make the majors and Heisman Trophy winners warm many an NFL bench. They've already won their prize.

Succeeding too early conveys a deceptive sense of entitlement. Not just Little League standouts but child movie stars and one-book authors often sink from sight. (A series of books called

Whatever Happened to . . . ? chronicled the quick fade of these bright young lights.) As with minor-league ballplayers who are brought up to the majors too soon, promotions bestowed too early in a career can rob those promoted of the drive they need to achieve lasting success. They're also not prepared for the pitfalls to come. "The only problem with success," said Tommy Lasorda, "is that it does not teach you how to deal with failure."

Success is at least as perilous as failure. It deprives us of motivation to make needed changes. Posttriumph, we have more to protect. That, in turn, makes it harder to sustain success. It's as hard or harder to remain successful as it is to succeed in the first place. Ask any coach. Just as weight can be more difficult to keep off than take off, prominent figures of all kinds discover that getting to the top is easier than staying there. "The toughest thing about success," said songwriter Irving Berlin, "is that you've got to keep on being a success." This is every bit as true of organizations as it is of persons. Like individuals, groups of people—teams, armies, corporations—routinely become victims of too much success.

5 · The Success Hobble

According to an old military axiom, *the weakest point always follows success*. At those times it's hard to resist the temptation to loosen up, take a breather, and abandon the intense concentration needed to fight your way up the next hill. Once a battle is won, soldiers are liable to ignore the sound of a twig snapping beneath the boot of an approaching scout, or overlook the glow of a distant campfire. Like soldiers, mountaineers say the most dangerous moment of their ascents is *after* they've reached the peak of a mountain. That's when they're most likely to fall into a crevasse or slip on a ledge. Surgeons, too, can find it difficult to stay focused once an operation has apparently succeeded. Until then, the demands of operating absorb their attention so completely that the scalpel seems almost to move itself.

The price of success too often is a loss of focus and daring. The tendency is to try to protect one's accomplishments by shifting into cruise control. This syndrome gets played out repeatedly in the television industry. One network climbs to the top, begins to play it safe, repeats what worked in the past, slips behind, then gives way to a competitor on the bottom who's taking creative chances because it has no reason not to.

Successful approaches don't just define what *can* be tackled, but what *can't*. That's how success inhibits flexibility and the ability to see what's on the horizon. Energy that's being poured into trying to duplicate past successes can't be applied to the search for new ones. This is a key reason that seeds of failure are routinely planted in the loam of organizational success. Doing too well breeds an excess of self-imitation. A culture of caution follows. In such a culture there's no reward and much penalty for taking chances. "If it ain't broke, don't fix it," becomes the mantra. It should be "If it ain't broke, fix it anyway!" In all likelihood, the formula for success that seems to be working fine is actually becoming extinct.

Doing things differently when the old ways are apparently working well defies logic. Yet, as IBM discovered, to survive in a changing economy that's exactly what must be done.

The Ashes of Success

IBM is a case study in the perils of success. For decades after World War II, IBM was the bluest of blue chips. Well into the 1980s, it made enormous amounts of money and was routinely judged America's most admired company by *Fortune*'s annual poll. In 1990, the computer behemoth enjoyed record profits. Two years later, it lost more money than any company in U.S. history. For a time, IBM teetered on the brink of collapse, along with the market for its dated computers and Selectric typewriters. While IBM had been busy earning so much money from the mainframes that had suited customers in the past, less successful companies were busily developing the smaller, more powerful, and affordable computers that would take over the future.

In its salad days, a management consultant asked one of IBM's mainframe managers about their development of a personal computer. "Why on earth would you care about the personal computer?" responded the executive. "It has nothing to do with office automation . . . in my opinion, we don't belong in the personal computer business to begin with." Even though IBM began developing a personal computer long before Jobs and Wozniak did, a workable version was still in development long after Apple II had come to market. Apple computers established such a firm beachhead that some of IBM's own product designers used them on the sly.

A maverick group of product developers in Boca Raton finally did get the IBM PC to market in late 1981. It was such a success that *IBM-compatible* became the industry standard for a few years after that. Its very success however, was the PC's undoing. When home office IBM executives realized how much money this product was making, they ordered its developers to emerge from their hideout in the Florida swamps and submit to Big Blue discipline. This meant spending years on the design of new products as various levels of bureaucracy signed off on any deviation from IBM's norms. The surest path to quick approval was to do things the way they had always been done. That process had worked well for mainframes. Wouldn't it work just as well for PCs?

Actually, no. After their initial success, the IBM PC developers routinely missed nearly every boat to come: clones, compacts, and networking. A few short years after its product conquered the personal computer market, IBM was reduced to being a bit player. Its personal computer division lost billions of dollars before finally returning to profitability in late 2000 on the strength of its ThinkPad laptops. The story of how IBM signed away billions of dollars in potential profits to operating system designer Bill Gates is legendary. Less well known is the fact that Mitch Kapor almost begged Big Blue to buy Lotus 1-2-3. Eventually, that spreadsheet program made Kapor wealthy. Veteran IBM watcher Paul Carroll of *The Wall Street Journal* thought that, if they hadn't missed this opportunity, the company could have dominated the PC market for years. IBM considered itself the world's software headquarters, however, and saw no need to step outside of channels and do business with an unconventional programmer who wore Hawaiian shirts.

Big Blue had its own way of doing things. One piece of IBM's own software was released with its e-mail function deleted because higher-ups wanted to reserve that feature for mainframes. If customers wanted e-mail on their PCs, they could buy a Compaq. That's exactly what many did.

The problem was that IBM enjoyed enormous profit margins even as the market for its products began to atrophy. This profitability suggested to IBM's product developers that they were on the right track, even when they were on the wrong one. "IBM's success made people feel they must be doing everything right," concluded Paul Carroll in his book *Big Blues,* "so why change anything?"

It wasn't always so. During IBM's start-up years, when it was a young upstart itself, then-Little Blue was more receptive to change, even change that might not succeed. If anything, they venerated failure. When a junior executive lost IBM $10 million on a risky venture, Tom Watson, Jr., rejected his offer to resign. "You can't be serious," said IBM's head. "We've just spent $10 million educating you!" Over time, however, the success Watson's company enjoyed with this philosophy made them reluctant to keep taking chances. At the peak of its success, IBM preferred to be second out of the gate with new products, or even third, but not first. Let someone else blaze trails. Rather than goading them to try new approaches, some high-profile failures (remember PCjr?) made IBM's culture more risk averse than ever. Big Blue's aversion to risking smaller failures nearly caused the big one: bankruptcy. It took some rough years in the mid-1990s and a CEO from the outside to jar IBM out of its postsuccess doldrums.

Nearly any apparent success can lead to failure if care isn't taken. IBM was hardly alone in that regard. Most profitable corporations get so committed to what's worked in the past that they can't expand their vision to consider what will work in the future. The modern histories of America's one-time most successful companies—IBM, Xerox, Eastman Kodak, Polaroid—read like the same story with interchangeable characters. The plots seldom vary. Like a huge army, a big company wins victories, dominates its market, gets bigger, develops rigid systems, resists change, then nearly succumbs to ragtag guerilla bands living off the land.

The list of those who didn't hear the rising drumbeat of the PC revolution reads like an all-star team of yesterday's successful technology companies: Texas Instruments did fabulously well at developing calculators, and remarkably badly at developing small computers. In the mid-1970s, Digital's CEO Kenneth Olsen discouraged development of a prototype home computer because he couldn't imagine that anybody would want one. Soon after that, Hewlett-Packard engineer Stephen Wozniak failed to interest his employer in the minicomputer he had designed, and instead developed that computer in the ranch home of Steve Jobs's parents.

Like football teams, organizations fall prey to their own winning record. Then, they must rebuild on the ashes of success. Some never do. Over and over again we see top corporations go from riches to rags in this way. Their problem is an excess of success. We're all prone to repeat what's worked in the past, even though it may not work in the future. No less than TV producers and football coaches, corporate managers face the nearly irresistible temptation to keep doing tomorrow what worked yesterday. This makes them backward looking rather than forward looking, stuck in a groove rather than cutting new trails. In the economy to come, what's worked in the past probably won't work in the future. Worse yet, it can blur our vision of what's on the horizon.

A company's inability to move beyond its current success is more often due to lack of vision than lack of opportunity. If Railway Express hadn't done so well shipping packages on trains it might have foreseen the demise of railroads and reinvented itself as Airway Express. Had Western Union not been so successful sending telegrams, they could have gotten into telephones instead of flower delivery. The telegraph company actually turned down an opportunity to develop Alexander Graham Bell's invention. As board member J. P. Morgan explained, Western Union considered the telephone little more than "an interesting novelty" that would never rival telegram sending. A few years later, the Remington Arms Company said they saw no future for a new "type-writing" machine because "no mere machine can replace a reliable and honest clerk."

IBM, A.B.Dick, and Eastman Kodak all declined Chester Carlson's offer to develop his newly invented dry photocopying method. Tiny Haloid finally bought Carlson's invention, then changed its name to Xerox. Within three decades, however, Xerox, too, became hobbled by its own success. In the annals of missed opportunities, Xerox is considered a hall of infamy. During the early 1970s, when Xerox's name was still synonymous with photocopying, researchers at its Palo Alto Research Center (PARC) developed the technology that made personal computers plausible. Their parent company was making so much money leasing copiers, however, that they saw no need to vigorously pursue this breakthrough. The graphical interface of Xerox's short-lived Alto computer later became the basis for user-friendly icons on Macs and Windows. Xerox subsequently ceded laser printer technology to Hewlett-Packard, desktop publishing to Adobe (a company founded by two ex-PARCers), and networking to Ethernet, also founded by a former Xerox employee. Jim Clark used research he did at PARC on 3-D graphical imaging to create Silicon Graphics. Another researcher took the what-you-see-is-what-you-get word-processing program he developed at Xerox to a more hospitable climate at Microsoft, which published it as Word. Other breakthroughs, developed at PARC but not exploited by its parent company, included the computer mouse and improvements of flat-panel displays. Xerox dealt itself a winning hand—several winning hands—then threw them in because it was reluctant to pursue innovations outside its core business. It was like a first-place major-league baseball team that develops one prospect after another, then releases them to become all-stars elsewhere. Xerox is a classic example of a business that was *too* successful.

As the technology revolution has illustrated time and time again, in today's economy innovations are best judged not only on immediate but also on long-term prospects. To companies such as Xerox, IBM, Hewlett-Packard, and Digital, personal computers had no obvious market. When compared with mainframes or even minicomputers, they offered too small a profit margin, too uncertain a customer base. This conflicted with the tried-and-true culture at such corporations. It took a completely new company like Apple to see opportunity where older, larger companies saw only risk.

Radical innovations can generally be relied upon to wreak havoc in risk-averse cultures long before they pay off. Companies that not only don't fear havoc, but thrive on it, are the ones best positioned to exploit breakthroughs. That price is far too high for those cruising in an if-it-ain't-broke-don't-fix-it mode. As Michael Lewis depicted in *The New New Thing,* when Jim Clark wanted Silicon Graphics to begin mass marketing desktop computers, the main problem he confronted was his own company's reluctance to undermine the bigger profit margins it was enjoying with larger computers. Clark faced a virtually impossible task: getting a company to make necessary but counterintuitive changes when it had a healthy bottom line. Every member of a profitable company is understandably invested in products that are making money. Undermining those products with new products that may have a smaller profit margin is not an idea that appeals to rational minds. In situations where we can't fathom what lies ahead, however, the value of logic wanes. Seemingly reasonable business procedures can be based on too many givens that may soon disappear. Then, we have to go beyond logic and rationality into a realm of counterintuitive daring. In such cases, it takes a bold mind like Jim Clark's, one comfortable with sometime irrationality, to swim upstream against the rushing waters of success.

An extraordinary amount of foresight, imagination, and will is required to rechart the course of big corporate ships with solid bottom lines. Yet, in a constantly changing marketplace, that is the only way to stay afloat. In principle, Digital could have morphed into an Apple, or Western Union into a Microsoft. There is no logical reason why one such industry can't segue into another. That type of radical reinvention almost never happens, however. Success in developing yesterday's cutting-edge technology seems almost to preclude an ability to develop tomorrow's. The amount of concentration it takes to make a go of one new product blinds us to others around the bend. Western Electric granted Sony the right to develop American-invented transistors because it didn't want to compete with its own lucrative vacuum tube business. Vacuum tubes soon succumbed to transistors, which then ceded their role to integrated circuits, semiconductors, and microprocessors. Manufacturers of microprocessors in turn overlooked their potential for personal computers. Personal-computer manufacturers may eventually give way to Internet boxes, or to some unforeseen breakthrough being developed in a teenager's garage. Developing a new product can call for giving up old ones that are still profitable.

An ability to prepare for the future may mean renouncing one's past success. As economist Lester Thurow has observed, "Businesses must be willing to destroy the old while it is still successful if they wish to build the new that will become successful." GE has made a near religion out of such "destroy your business" thinking. So have other farsighted companies. It isn't easy. Innovation never is.

Roads Best Not Taken

No matter how much they crave innovation in principle, most corporations are risk averse at heart. Too often, their managers resort to tactics that look as though they might promote innovation, but probably won't, because they involve no real risk, no fundamental change. Like a Harley-riding CEO, such tactics give the illusion of dynamic change without much substance. These strategies are based on old paradigms of success and failure. They include:

1. EXHORTATION. Exhorting employees in speeches, memos, and e-mail to be bolder, take more risks, and be more entrepreneurial seldom accomplishes anything of the sort. Pleading with employees to "take more risks!" is like admonishing a slumping batter to "get more hits!" Those exhorted usually know they should be bolder, but they sense, usually accurately, that no matter how much they're encouraged to take more chances, most settings offer far greater rewards for playing it safe. Shrewd employees realize that behind every plea to take more risk is the implied corollary: "Just be sure they succeed." In the words of one middle manager, "They keep telling us to take more risks, but you're expected never to fail."

2. TWEAKING. This is an unusually seductive approach: making cosmetic changes that give the appearance of dynamic

change without requiring any fundamental revision in the way business gets done. Sending employees to seminars on innovation. Hiring consultants to create new corporate names and logos. Offering cappuccino in the commissary. Some staid organizations note that livelier ones have a lot of scruffy employees who can sometimes be seen throwing Frisbees outside company headquarters. Hence, they loosen their dress codes and encourage employees to be more playful. Without a deep and genuine interest in promoting change, such cosmetic efforts seldom have the desired effect. It's like saying that the pantaloons worn by Cossacks was what made them such fierce warriors.

3. CONQUEST. McDonald's Ray Kroc once said that if he came upon a competitor drowning, he would stick a hose in his mouth. That was success on the combat model: No quarter! Knocking off Burger King would be the biggest success of all. Success isn't defined this way in an economy based on collaboration as much as competition. These days, it's not always clear who your opponent is. A competitor in one area is a partner in another. Today's foe is tomorrow's ally. That can vary from one situation to another, and change over time. Competition gives way to coopetition: competing in some areas, cooperating in others. This hardly means companies no longer compete, simply that they don't try to eliminate an opponent whose services might be useful to them in the future. During Microsoft's antitrust trial, it was striking how many bitter rivals had either partnered with Bill Gates's behemoth on specific projects, or tried to. Microsoft itself wisely invested in a troubled Apple to help keep it alive. Exterminating such an opponent could

kill off a valuable potential ally. Today's economy requires a much more complex, ambiguous form of success.

4. INCENTIVES. One of management's most hallowed concepts is that employee accomplishments should be rewarded with trophies, bonuses, preferred parking places, and box seats at baseball games. Couldn't the same approach encourage innovation? Actually, it's more likely to have the opposite effect. Research has shown repeatedly that those motivated by the prospect of a prize approach their work in rote fashion. Prize winning becomes the goal, not trying something different. Considering a new approach, playing a hunch, taking extra time to exceed expectations all make it less likely that we'll win a trophy. Awards are usually given to those who work well on existing terms. Trophies generally end up on the mantles of those who play it safe, not the ones who take a chance. As social critic Alfie Kohn noted in his book *Punished by Rewards,* prizes discourage risk taking. When working for a prize, we do only what's necessary to win it. Kohn quoted one advocate of pay-for-performance programs who observed, without irony, that "People will do precisely what they are asked to do, if the reward is significant." There's no better way to discourage innovation. The manager's job isn't to guess what prizes will reward success best. It's to figure out how to make jobs so satisfying and so challenging that doing them well becomes its own reward.

5. PERFORMANCE REVIEW. During a performance review, not just criticism but praise can demotivate. Praise too easily becomes perfunctory, manipulative, and insincere. It's a first-rate

conversation ender. ("Keep up the good work.") Like any reward, praise motivates us to seek external reinforcement for a job well done, rather than developing high standards of our own. It can also raise the bar of expectations in unproductive ways. As Alfie Kohn put it, "Praise sets up unrealistic expectations of continued success, which leads people to avoid difficult tasks in order not to risk the possibility of failure." That's one reason performance reviews, including favorable ones, are so dreaded by manager and employee alike. Even when a review is positive and the news is all good, an atmosphere of judgment continues to do damage. Introducing a judgmental attitude severely inhibits their relationship. When one person evaluates another, there's little possibility that either can be open. Small wonder that studies repeatedly find no correlation exists between productivity and performance reviews.

6. STANDARDIZED MEASURES. When institutionwide performance reviews are based on standardized measures, added problems arise. These tests are based on old models of success and failure. They arbitrarily create win–lose categories. The more we employ standardized measures to evaluate achievement, the more arbitrary our so-called victories and defeats become. What's meant to be a diagnostic tool becomes a source of reward or penalty. ("How did we do on the test?") This promotes unproductive rivalry. In educational systems, pitting one school district against another in terms of students' test scores has resulted in widespread cheating to raise those scores. The use of standardized tests also promotes teaching to the test, adding unproductive stress to education. The fact that they're so test-bound is one reason failure is such a taboo in so many European and Asian

societies. The irony is that America is trying to become more like them just as they're trying to become more like America. Former Labor Secretary Robert Reich has called the growing trend toward standardized testing ". . . . [M]onstrously unfair to many kids. We're creating a one-size-fits-all system that needlessly brands many young people as failures, when they might thrive if offered a different education whose progress was measured differently. Paradoxically, we're embracing standardized tests just when the new economy is eliminating standardized jobs."

7. ACCOUNTABILITY. Accountability is supposed to improve productivity by tracking performance. Up to a point, like most well-intended management expectations, this one may have the desired effect. In the long run, however, there could hardly be a more inhibiting practice. When made a fetish, accountability stifles creativity. Far from making employees perform better long term, accountability encourages a culture of evasion, denial, and finger pointing. ("It was *her* fault, not mine.") The result is something less than an innovative atmosphere. Even though employees should be held to their commitments, making accountability the focus of one's management style is a surefire way to make them run for cover. As Ambrose Bierce recognized a century ago, accountability is "the mother of caution." On its watch, when things go wrong, we want to assign individual blame. Just as credit for success is best passed around, however, blame for failure should also be shared. An enlightened company such as Southwest Airlines takes a nonpunitive, team approach to dealing with delayed flights, looking not for culprits to punish but lessons to learn. The result? Southwest has the quickest

turnaround time in the industry: twenty minutes, on the average, to unload a plane, clean it up, reload, and be ready for takeoff.

8. PLANS. An old homily has it that *failing to plan is planning to fail.* Like so many homilies, this one contains a kernel of truth. One hardly wants to embark on new ventures half-cocked. It's understandable to assume that departures in the way companies do business should be carefully planned. Understandable, but not always accurate. Serious innovation doesn't lend itself to conventional business plans. Such plans imply some ability to forecast the future. This ability is not only rare to nonexistent, but the very idea that we can see ahead is downright dangerous. It blinds us to events that are actually emerging. The best way to discover how to take advantage of the future is by employing methods that are as disorderly as life itself. Capital One revolutionized the credit-card industry by doing thousands of mailings a year that pitched cards to niche markets with an ever-changing constellation of interest rates, bonus offers, and other incentives, then using its mistakes to determine which pitches worked and which didn't. The company knew in advance that most of its new approaches would fail. But, as Capital One's cofounder Richard Fairbank told *The New Yorker*'s James Surowiecki, "Failure is information, too." Some call this approach "enlightened trial and error." In a world changing as rapidly as ours is, trial and error may be the best, perhaps the *only,* way to identify emerging markets. Even though so-called error is the more likely outcome of any trial, error making should hardly be equated with failure. "We are all in a continuing dialogue with the world," said Monsanto's Robert Shapiro, "and the world tells you what it wants.

When it tells you that what you offer isn't what it wants, you haven't failed. You've moved one step closer to learning about the world."

9. ACQUISITION. Big, established companies often try to jump-start the innovation process by letting small start-ups innovate, then acquiring them. Sometimes this works. Too often, however, putting those small companies and their daredevil employees in a risk-averse culture is like planting palm trees in Siberia and hoping they'll survive. Mattel nearly scuttled itself by trying to incorporate Learning Co. into its more conventional culture. Innovating through acquisition is more likely to blur focus than promote change. Energy gets diverted into blending cultures with all the attendant turf protection and tribal strife. Such conflict can tap enormous reserves of creativity, but not productive ones. Innovation by acquisition also makes big companies that much bigger and less receptive to new approaches. In yesterday's economy, size was a symbol of success. ("IBM is big, but bigger we will be," bragged their company anthem.) In today's economy, size can be a serious impediment to needed innovation. Smaller companies are better able to offer their members an opportunity to take risks, including ones that don't pan out, on a manageable scale.

10. INCUBATION. A more promising, but still problematic, approach is to foster innovation by creating *incubators:* small, protected ventures within large ones where creative minds can play it loose. This approach dates back at least to Lockheed's postwar Skunkworks, which produced the Stealth fighter, among other

things. As the occasional success of such ventures indicates, they don't lack merit, but creating innovative oases in a desert that's hostile to their presence seldom accomplishes its overall goal. If entrenched members of the old order remain in a position to sabotage skunkworkers, the skunkworkers might as well have not been hired in the first place. Xerox's PARC researchers came up with one brilliant innovation after another, only to see them get shelved by a company that didn't welcome any real departure from what it was already doing. Making a companywide commitment to innovate would have been more effective than confining innovation to its Palo Alto incubator. Even when incubators do succeed, their success comes at a price. That price is to segregate an organization's most fertile minds into ghettos of innovation. The real goal should be to infuse the entire organization with an innovative spirit rather than to isolate its most fertile minds. Make every department a skunkworks. The more desirable approach is to innovate throughout a company's culture, and in the process make it more receptive to any useful change.

Don't Just Survive

Only systems that evolve continually can compete in a constantly changing economy. As with an endangered species whose habitat is disappearing, discovering a new habitat is essential for the continued health of even flourishing companies. This is why so many economists believe innovations that alter the way companies do business are actually more valuable—dollars-and-cents valuable—than any hardware or software they can buy. Such reinvention could fail, of course. There's the rub. A company that's enjoying marketplace success, and has profit centers to protect, doesn't *want* to risk more than the most insignificant kinds of failure. Anything more would feel like asking a .400 batter to start swinging from the other side of the plate. This kind of fundamental change would require transforming their corporate-culture habitat completely. That's exactly what's necessary.

Most organizations equate success with *survival.* These include not only the old IBM but universities, foundations, and government agencies. Private industries have a more complicated mission. Their survival depends on making profits. Those profits could vanish overnight, and probably will, if they rely on what's worked in the past. When the world is changing so rapidly around them, not to change is to commit suicide. Healthy organizations in the future will be constantly self-scrutinizing, continually self-renewing, regularly overhauling their culture. Their reinvention must be nonstop. Things move too fast now to postpone this process.

The most farsighted corporations reinvent their cultures before they are forced to. They know this road will be bumpy, not clearly successful in conventional terms. Accepting setbacks as the price of innovation is central to the way new managers of old companies try to emulate the startups that are nibbling away at their foundations. This is not simply a question of managers versus entrepreneurs, established companies versus start-ups, or small organizations taking on big ones. Companies such as Motorola, Intel, and GE reinvent themselves continually. (Motorola's motto reflects this attitude: *Renewing a renewed organization.*) They distrust apparent success, and begin to transform themselves once again as soon as a renewal cycle is completed. In the ever-renewing company, there is no such thing as success in the static sense, only as an ongoing process. Even when a transformation is apparently successful, it is viewed not as an episode but as a never-completed story. Success in such settings is always a journey, never a destination. There, innovation is nonstop.

6 · Innovating with Attitude

The popular conception of innovation is that it's highly desirable but rare and difficult to elicit. Actually, it's the other way around. The problem is not an idea shortage. New approaches can usually be elicited just by asking for them. The average brainstorming session produces lots of fresh thinking. Good ideas surround us. Openness to such ideas does not. What's at a premium is *receptivity* to innovative suggestions and the vision to pursue them, even if that means reconceiving altogether what we're up to. For companies that were slow to make effective use of the Internet, the problem was not technological ignorance or lack of resources, it was lack of imagination. They were thinking about office networks while their customers were dreaming of global communications. Innovation does not result from changes in management technique or the purchase of cutting-edge technology. The key is openness.

The best ideas aren't hidden in shadowy recesses. They're right in front of us, hidden in plain sight. Innovation seldom depends on discovering obscure or subtle elements but in seeing the obvious with fresh eyes. This is easier said than done, because nothing is as hard to see as what's right before our eyes. We overlook what we take for granted. Billions of tea drinkers observed the force of steam escaping from water boiling in a kettle before James Watt realized that this vapor could be converted into energy. Others who worked with penicillium mold knew that bacteria didn't grow around it, but it took Alexander Flemming to recognize that *it killed bacteria*! Could penicillium be used to fight infection? That obvious question, ignored by everyone else, gave birth to the field of antibiotics.

Those who see what's obvious aren't necessarily brighter than others. They're just more likely to observe that the emperor is naked. Like children, they see what's actually there. Their perceptions are less clouded by belief systems, taboos, habits of thought. One responsibility of management—an important one—is to call attention to the invisible obvious, pointing it out as a child does (sometimes to the embarrassment of adults). Doing so also requires supporting employees who take that risk, too, and other risks as well.

The Risk-Friendly Workplace

Hiring risk takers is only a first step on the innovation trail. Creating an environment in which innovators can flourish is the next, far harder, step. Much more effective than exhorting employees to take more risks is creating a risk-friendly working environment. Most employees don't avoid risk because they're dumb, ignorant, or cowardly. They know well enough what it means to take a chance. Under the right circumstances, they might like to do so. But those who work in settings that are too success obsessed hunker down and avoid doing anything that could detract from succeeding on conventional terms. In this context, employees don't welcome innovation and certainly wouldn't want to initiate it.

If we want to encourage genuine risk taking—the only sure

path to actual innovation—we first must reduce apprehension about making mistakes. "Punishing failure assures that no one dares," said Jack Welch. Under Welch, General Electric sometimes even rewarded failure. In one case, some GE product developers who came up with a new lamp design that didn't pan out were given television sets. Without such gestures of unmistakable failure tolerance, said Welch, "people will be afraid to try things."

When an organization wants to become more accommodating of actual risk taking, it needs to convey that its commitment to change goes beyond lip service. Creating a risk-friendly environment requires demonstrating unequivocally, in deeds more than words, that stumbles on the innovation path are forgiven. How better for managers to achieve this end than by publicizing their own missteps? If we want employees to admit their mistakes, we had better admit our own. If we want them to risk failure, we won't stonewall our own lost risks. As David Greising pointed out in *I'd Like the World to Buy a Coke*, Roberto Goizueta got years of one liners out of reactions to his New Coke fiasco, such as the irate letter he received from a classic Coke lover that began, "Dear Chairman Dodo." Admitting this conveyed better than a hundred speeches or a thousand memos that risk taking was genuinely in order.

A former Lockheed executive recalled the time CEO Dan Houghton gathered his company's manufacturing heads to discuss his own errors. Howard Hughes had once called to tell Houghton that Douglas Aircraft was in trouble and he should get right over there and buy it "before Jimmy McDonnell does." Houghton told his managers that not taking Hughes's advice was the biggest blunder he had made in business. Had he done so, Lockheed could have consolidated its operations in Southern California and avoided costly future moves. According to the former Lockheed executive, he and his colleagues left this meeting not only with increased respect for Houghton but renewed motivation to take chances of their own. He had told them in the most eloquent way that losing a gamble wasn't the worst thing that could happen to them. The message their CEO conveyed was: "If Dan Houghton can make mistakes, I guess I can, too."

Sprinters and Milers

We can't expect all employees to be innovative and wouldn't want them to be. Armies need soldiers as well as scouts. What we can do is try to keep those who aren't innovative out of the way of those who are. Organizations harbor, and need, both types of employee. Most working environments include both sprinters and milers. (At Microsoft they're called "pioneers and settlers.") One innovates, the other consolidates. Effective managers want both on their team, just not in the same position. Milers are absolutely essential for the long-term health and stability of any organization. They pace themselves, take the long view, and provide a steady hand on the tiller of their boats. Established companies are the natural habitat of milers. Sprinters, on the other hand, are any organization's main source of innovation. The tried and true bores them. Change excites them. Miler-oriented companies need to accommodate sprinters. In a constantly changing economy, their presence has become, paradoxically, essential for long-term organizational health.

Accommodating sprinters goes well beyond allowing them to

wear t-shirts to work and keep cats in their cubicles. By themselves, pay raises and perks are virtually worthless to novelty seekers. Dire warnings that start-ups might fail are no more effective with those who find this prospect intriguing than is telling teenagers that loud music could damage their hearing. Both know; neither cares. Better to offer sprinters an opportunity to make more money with more risk, accept their surreptitious activities, allow them to make decisions based on incomplete information, without having to back up every proposal with detailed research, and let them run with promising, if uncertain, ideas. In other words, behave entrepreneurially within a bureaucracy. A start-up mentality can be encouraged within existing organizations by creating small, semiautonomous operations buffered from inevitable attempts at sabotage by milers. Such ventures may not attract actual pirates, but they will appeal to privateers who like to take chances as long as they have the safety net of an established company's resources. That's a valuable type of employee to have, but not always an affable one. Great achievers seldom are.

Wild Ducks

Innovators are seldom easy to be around. The most creative members of an organization can be irascible, annoying, touchy, intolerant, prickly, self-aggrandizing. Their lack of tact offends coworkers. It also makes them willing to speak up when others hold their tongues. What comes out of their mouths is often quite valuable, if not always easy to hear.

At a California Internet start-up, most employees realized

that the ideas expressed by its leading technology expert were right more often than wrong. Unfortunately, his thoughts were conveyed in such an irritating and abrasive way that coworkers attacked him continually. More time and energy were spent trying to isolate this man than to benefit from his suggestions. In the process his company was deprived of one of its most creative resources. A similar process contributed to Xerox's inability to exploit PARC's discoveries. In *Dealers of Lightning*, a history of PARC, author Michael Hitzick concluded that the "alien habits of mind and behavior" of its inventors were part of the reason Xerox didn't pay enough attention to their inventions.

One source of IBM's early prowess was the fact that both Tom Watson, Sr. and Jr., made good use of *wild ducks:* those who refused to fly in formation. Tom Watson, Jr., filled key positions with "harsh, scratchy people" who were not afraid to speak their minds. These mavericks had much to do with IBM's success. The Watsons' successors didn't share their taste for birds out of formation, however. In time, IBM's most independent minds were rebuked, isolated, even forced out of the company. It's not entirely coincidental that this intolerance of prickly innovators coincided with the company's decline.

Nonconformists are no more popular in most workplaces than they were in high school. Management's task is to create an environment that's receptive to whoever makes a contribution, whether they're popular or not. Unorthodox, difficult, imaginative employees must be retained because innovation depends upon their creativity. Organizations that want more innovation are utterly dependent on difficult individuals. They're the ones who come up with novel approaches overlooked by more prudent colleagues.

Economist Paul Romer, who theorized that innovation was central to wealth creation, went so far as to conclude that "A certain tolerance for nonconformism is really critical to the process."

One of management's most important duties is to protect innovators who march to their own drummer (straight across coworkers' turfs) from outraged colleagues who have a better sense of how the game is usually played. Part of any manager's job description is acting as a bodyguard for irascible innovators. Their ventures must be protected from a broader culture that doesn't necessarily wish them well. In time the broader culture may find itself nourished by the presence of these feisty microbes. A neo-entrepreneurial atmosphere could follow, one that accommodates all kinds of personalities and all manner of mistake making. It has at 3M.

Minnesota Mining and Mistake Making

Post-it Notes are the result of a mistake. That mistake was made in 1968 by 3M scientist Spencer Silver, who was trying to develop an unusually strong adhesive. One batch of Silver's experimental glue was unusually weak. Silver told 3M colleagues about his low-adhesive glue in hopes that they would find a use for it. Years later, another 3M scientist, Art Fry, sat in church, reflecting on his colleague's false start. As he reflected, Fry struggled to keep paper bookmarks from falling out of his hymnal. Two and two converged in his mind. Fry recalled that a unique property of Silver's weak glue was its ability to readhere once pulled loose. Suppose it were applied to bookmarks or other kinds of paper? Could small pieces of paper be stuck and restuck to other surfaces? It turned out they could. In 1980, six years after Fry's divine inspiration, Post-it Notes appeared on the market. They went on to become one of 3M's biggest moneymakers. In offices around the world, this product leads the list of *how-did-we-ever-get-along-without?* inventions.

3M is like a shrine of products developed by accident. A failed bra cup became a successful surgeon's mask. So-so surgical tape morphed into superb household tape. Scotchgard was discovered after a 3M chemist spilled a fluorochemical on her sneakers and found it shed the water she used to try to get it off.

A 3M executive once admitted that they were a bit embarrassed by how many of their successful products resulted from happy accidents rather than deliberate research. That misses the point. Accidents occur every day in all organizations. Usually they're ignored, or hushed up. At 3M, Spencer Silver spread the word about his goof in hopes someone else might find a way to use it. Art Fry did.

3M's approach has always been one of two steps forward, one step back. Even those not working on product development are encouraged to be more imaginative through inspirational tales about those who are. The company's culture is conveyed through storytelling, mythmaking, and icon worship. Innovators such as Fry and Silver are lionized. Stories depicting how products such as masking tape and Thinsulate survived internal attempts to do them in are told and retold around corporate campfires.

Resistance to the termination of projects is central to 3M lore. "It's better to seek forgiveness than to ask for permission," has long been a credo of the company's product developers. The tangible results of that attitude are less important than the atmosphere it creates: one of top-to-bottom support for fiddling around that might lead somewhere. Covert research by 3Mers is winked at. *Bootleggers*—those who surreptitiously keep new-product programs alive after they were supposed to have died—are the bad boys everyone loves at 3M. Lewis Lehr became a corporate legend by ignoring an order to stop producing the surgical drapes that eventually became a big moneymaker. Because it tolerates mavericks, 3M attracts mavericks. "We don't even need to look for them," explained Lehr after becoming 3M's CEO. "They'll find us if we let them."

In our volatile economy, anointing paragons is a risky business. At this writing, however, 3M exemplifies as well as any company the relationship between innovation and mistake tolerance, and has for decades. This company's very existence is due to a blunder. Minnesota Mining and Manufacturing was founded at the turn of the century to mine an abrasive called *corundum.* Their mine turned out to have no usable corundum, however, or valuable minerals of any kind. In 1905, the company turned its attention to producing sandpaper. The results were so bad that 3M's president didn't draw a paycheck for over a decade. A factory the company built in 1910 collapsed before it was operational. It wasn't until 1916, fourteen years after its founding, that 3M paid shareholders a dividend.

From the rubble of this disastrous beginning, however, grew a company that could be the most consistently innovative business in American history. One is related to the other. In *The 3M Way to Innovation,* his excellent study of 3M's culture, management consultant Ernest Gundling concluded, "Perhaps the adversity 3M faced during those [early] years helped to make it the innovative company that it is today, for it served to teach the employees then and now a valuable lesson: success can emerge from failure."

Ever since Thomas Peters and Robert Waterman sang 3M's praises in *In Search of Excellence,* the company has hosted a stream of visitors from other companies who want to benchmark their approach to innovation. "What's the secret?" they ask. Is it their high research and development budget? The fact that product developers can spend up to 15 percent of their time on their own projects? The expectation that 30 percent of all 3M products should be ones that didn't exist four years earlier? The so-called Eleventh Commandment, "Thou shalt not kill a new product idea," with the burden of proof placed on idea killers? The many semiautonomous divisions 3M harbors? Its strong, enlightened leadership? Or is it 3M's Pacing Plus program that subsidizes promising new programs with modest grants?

What's the key?

Visitors are told that it's all of the above, and none of the above. What matters more than any checklist of programs is an atmosphere in which 3Mers feel that it's okay to try something new because they won't be hung out to dry if it doesn't pan out. Without such an atmosphere, any specific innovation-encouraging policy is meaningless. A receptive attitude matters more than any program. Visitors leaving with that message usually look disappointed. They came looking for policies and programs to transplant to their own companies, not culture and climate. Yet the latter, what Ernest Gundling calls "the complex fabric of success and failure," is more important than any other part of 3M's innovation equation.

3M executives recognize that innovation has more to do with anthropology than technology. If an organization's culture supports, genuinely supports, new approaches, such approaches will emerge like revelers on New Year's Eve. If it only pays lip service to innovation, however, savvy employees will hunker down. When that happens, no amount of exhortation, no new organizational chart, or piece of sophisticated software will contribute an iota to innovation.

If ever a company has taken seriously the admonition to pursue success by doubling failures, it's 3M. This company estimates that 60 percent of its formal new-product programs go belly up. "When this happens," said Lewis Lehr, "the important thing is not to crucify the people on the project. They should know that their jobs with the company are not in jeopardy if they fail. Otherwise, too many would-be innovators will give in to the quite natural temptation to play it safe." Managers reinforce 3M's mistake-tolerant atmosphere by freely admitting their own goofs. Lehr's successor, L. D. DeSimone, never hesitated to recount how often he tried to stop the development of Thinsulate. Luckily, DeSimone failed, and Thinsulate—the lightweight insulator that can be found in so many garments, shoes, and sleeping bags—became one of 3M's most successful products. By being so candid about his near blunder, DeSimone told 3Mers in the most eloquent terms that it's okay to be wrong, and even better to admit being wrong.

The sense that innovation includes goofing up permeates 3M's culture. Its product developers haven't just been lucky. Nor are they necessarily more creative than counterparts at other companies. Managers have simply been more receptive to the idea that a company can literally profit from its own mistakes. A fifty-year-old statement of philosophy made by then-CEO William McKnight is continually quoted at 3M: "Mistakes will be made, but if a person is essentially right, the mistakes he or she makes are not as serious, in the long run, as the mistakes management will make if it's dictatorial and undertakes to tell those under its authority exactly how they must do their job."

To be this mistake tolerant requires a certain mindset. At the heart of this mindset is a recognition that success can't be divorced from failure. This does not call for celebrating each and every failure. All failures are not created equal, and some should hardly be celebrated. However, a willingness to examine setbacks—and successes—to see what can be learned from them is at the heart of enlightened management. Managers who take this approach go beyond success and failure, into a realm that might be called postfailure.

7 · Managing in the Postfailure Era

In rapidly changing times, it's impossible to know what unforeseen circumstances may alter one's plans. Projects seldom, if ever, work out as planned. Some companies incorporate exit strategies into each new venture because they know and accept that many will fail. Others launch two or more projects with the same goal, going in different directions simultaneously. This approach not only provides options midway through the process, but also creates two different crops that can crossfertilize each other. In a conventional sense, one approach fails when the other reaches a goal first. But does the word *failure* really apply? Both approaches—the one that succeeded and the one that didn't—were interdependent from the outset.

Such *simultaneous management* (the title of a book on this subject by Alexander Laufer) is just one way to manage effectively in the postfailure era. There are many more, including *enlightened trial and error.* All such approaches require setting aside simplistic notions about failure and success. That's what we mean by postfailure management. Like David Levy's boss at Apple, some managers urge employees to fail more. That doesn't sound too hard. One would think failure was easy enough to come by. What isn't easy is getting employees to take the kinds of risks that might fail. It takes a special and unusual management attitude to encourage prudent employees to risk making a mistake.

During his years at Monsanto, Robert Shapiro was impressed by how terrified most employees were of failing. They had been trained to see the failure of a product as a personal rebuke. Shapiro tried to break that connection. Every product was an experiment, he said. Its backers failed only if their experiment was poorly designed. This approach made an important distinction between excusable and inexcusable failure. A half-hearted, careless effort with lame results is inexcusable. A deliberate, well-thought-out effort that didn't succeed isn't. That type of failure is not only excusable but desirable.

There are failures and failures. Some can be lethal—producing and marketing a dysfunctional tire, for example. At no time can management be casual about issues of health and safety. Encouragement of failure doesn't mean the abandonment of supervision, quality control, or respect for sound practices. Just the opposite. Postfailure management requires *more* engagement with the process, not less. Despite the inevitability of mistakes when launching new ventures, management cannot abdicate its responsibility to assess the nature of the failures it encounters. Some are excusable mistakes on the path to innovation. Others aren't. Criteria for distinguishing between excusable and inexcusable mistakes include:

- Did the employee design this project conscientiously or was it carelessly organized?
- Could the failure have been prevented if necessary research or consultation had been accomplished properly?

- Was the project conducted in a spirit of collaboration, or did the employee ignore input from others who could have helped, or fail to check with colleagues who should have been informed?
- Did the project fail because it was burdened by requirements that weren't germane to the actual goal, but served only to meet personal needs of the employee?
- Were there clear instances of deception with respect to projections of risks, costs, time, and so on, or were variations from projections the result of honest mistakes?
- Was the mistake in question committed repeatedly?

The essence of postfailure management is identifying excusable failure and approaching it as an important part of the innovation process to be examined, understood, and built upon. Success can be approached in much the same way. Just as enlightened managers don't ignore failure but regard it as a potential step on the road to success, success is not celebrated as final, but regarded as a step on the road to more creative failures.

Like mistakes, all successes are not created equal. A success due to a fortunate accident is not on the same plane as one that results from years of conscientious effort. Apparent successes might be evaluated with questions similar to those posed about failures. How much was due to good fortune, how much to the hard work of its creator? Were all contributors acknowledged? Did the success move us closer to our goals? Will it actually serve our customers' needs or simply merit an award from our peers?

By taking this perspective and raising such questions, managers can begin to treat success and failure similarly, more like the siblings they actually are.

Treating Success and Failure Alike

The very terms *success* and *failure* are used sparingly in the lexicon of enlightened managers. They understand that rewarding one and punishing the other can create more problems than it solves. Therefore, they approach them both with the same posture.

That can be a difficult idea to embrace. Treat them the same? It's hard not to wonder, "Shouldn't I recognize a success with an award, or at least some praise? And even if I don't reprimand an employee's failure, shouldn't I at least ignore and overlook it?"

Well, no. We suggest a different approach. During Olympic volleyball games, after each point, win or lose, teammates commonly shake hands with one another. Whether the players make the shot or miss, they are given the support and appreciation of the others. They treat failure and success the same way. We take that as a kind of metaphor for good management.

Good coaches take victory and defeat in stride. "I didn't get consumed by losses," said Don Shula, "and I didn't get overwhelmed by successes." We suggest the same strategy for managers. The best managers already do this. Rather than pursue "success," they focus on increasing their organization's intellectual capital: the experience, knowledge, and creativity of its workforce. How is this done? Through *engagement*. In place of perfunctory compliments or withering criticism, they take a tangible interest in the work of employees. They get involved.

Instead of simply evaluating their employees' efforts, they try to understand the work, interpret it, and discover its meaning to the employee. Often, they are in a position to see the work in a larger context, to put a bigger frame around it. They can discuss a project's history, its goals, where it's located on the organization's larger map, the underlying methods employed, the technology involved, and the next steps an employee might take.

This process is more collaborative than supervisory in spirit. Good managers show interest, express support, ask pertinent questions: What's new with your project? What kinds of problems are you having? By using this color scheme, did you intend to connect the product with our previous line? Or did you have a new market in mind altogether? Let's take the long view and imagine what direction your project might take. Where should we go from here? What do you see as the next steps?

In such conversations, whether the project succeeded or failed is less important than what can be learned from the experience. When a manager and employee are deeply engaged in this discussion, both enter the same kind of zone that athletes do. In this zone, evaluation is less relevant than the question of where to go from here—a better question than whether the project "succeeded" or "failed."

Over time, conversations such as these create a new working environment, one that invites innovation by redefining success and failure. This does not mean there should be no applause for a major achievement, or that repeated, avoidable mistakes should be tolerated. Well-intended and carefully planned efforts that produce mistakes are recognized as such, however, and treated as stumbles due to vigorous effort.

Through this kind of involvement, effective managers give *themselves*. Listening is more central to this process than talking. Innovation-encouraging managers motivate employees by taking a genuine interest in their work. Research on workplace creativity shows that it's not freedom as much as the involvement of management that produces creative acts. No incentive can match the obvious appreciation shown by a manager's enthusiasm. Pathbreaking leaders such as Edison, Kettering, the Watsons, and 3M's William McKnight were famous for schmoozing with employees—not second-guessing or criticizing but engaging in animated discussion about their projects. Nothing does more for productivity, morale, and employee retention. "Edison made your work interesting," said a machinist and draftsman who spent a half-century working for the inventor. "He made me feel that I was making something with him. I wasn't just a workman."

New approaches are most likely to emerge in the workplace when *involved* managers discard obsolete norms of success and failure, and treat steps in the innovation process—those that work and those that don't—much the same, with less evaluation and more interpretation. In other words, they don't penalize; they *analyze*. When he ran Allied Signal, Lawrence Bossidy told *The New York Times* that, even though he liked to hire managers who had experienced failure, this didn't mean he wanted to praise setbacks, or criticize them, for that matter. Even major failures were best handled by analysis, Bossidy thought. Why did it happen? What can be learned from this experience? Sometimes, this involved admitting that he himself was part of a failed project. Then, the message became, "Now, let's make sure we don't make that same mistake again when we develop another product."

In place of external incentives or sanctions, engaged managers get to know their employees' ideas, their problems, their frustrations, their hopes. Instead of criticizing or praising, they strive to understand better what their employees are up to. Less praise? Haven't managers been told not to skimp on compliments? They have indeed. But psychologists who have studied the effects of praise question its value. As with criticism, compliments can actually demotivate. They can make recipients feel manipulated or think that too much is expected of them. Research has found that children playing games lose interest once they're rewarded for their play, even by compliments. In one study, students praised less by science teachers did a better job of conducting experiments on their own than ones who were praised more. This is why, in place of perfunctory praise, many educators are shifting to a teaching style in which they ask questions, give feedback, and show interest, but are sparing with compliments. "That's great!" gives way to "I see you've decided to use liquid nitrogen in this experiment." A specific response like that shows real interest in a student's work. It's appreciated more than expected praise. Genuine engagement is a better motivator than routine compliments.

In the workplace, praise can become what is called a *dissatisfier*. Like a salary, it is less likely to motivate when given than demotivate when it's expected but withheld. So, managers cannot suddenly abandon the practice of praising those who have come to expect it. When they become genuinely engaged with the employee's work, however, the need for compliments declines.

Like better teachers, engaged managers realize the value of taking a tangible interest in the work of their employees. This is easier said than done. Genuine engagement can require far more time than the eleven minutes managers spend per task, on average. Since such involvement takes more time than keeping your distance, occasions for doing so must be chosen carefully. Engaging with employees is demanding and risky. It could threaten a manager's authority. The more involved managers get with employees, the harder it becomes to reprimand them, if necessary. Although not the same as personal friendships, engaged professional relationships resemble them in ways that can hinder the supervisory process. Wisdom consists of learning how to become closely involved with the work of an employee without becoming pals.

One reason managers may be wary of this type of engagement is that it can be unpredictable, raising questions they might rather avoid. By the same token, the very open-ended, less formal nature of an engaged relationship can lead to the type of unexplored terrain where innovation lies. This treacherous terrain is where the biggest successes and failures take place. Engaged managers get involved with those who have experienced either one, and treat both as steps toward achievement to be studied, understood, and built upon.

Earning Empathy

Earlier, we discussed the value of admitting mistakes for conveying the idea that mistake making is in order. Far from revealing weakness, doing this suggests that a leader is self-confident enough to admit a mistake. It has the added value of forging closer ties to employees and colleagues. A blunder admitted is empathy earned. Leaders who don't cover up their own setbacks become people whom others can not only admire but with whom they can identify.

When a group of employees recalled what experiences with their bosses were most important to them, nearly every memory involved an occasion when the boss's facade cracked, and he or she was revealed as a human being. One fledgling paramedic felt better when his supervisor admitted that, after thirty years on the job, she still got scared. A young professor couldn't get along with his dean until that man confessed how frustrating his career had been. After that, he approached the dean with a more understanding, cooperative attitude.

Knowing that leaders have stumbled reveals them as human, too, and enhances their ability to lead. Since setbacks are so much more universal than successes, we respond best to leaders who—like us—have experienced failure. Think Truman. Think Lincoln. Think Grant. Ulysses S. Grant's success as a military officer grew directly out of his problems as a civilian. Grant's drinking problem made him more sympathetic to the weakness of others. His struggle to control himself helped him understand discipline issues with subordinates. The humiliation of failing repeatedly in business not only made Grant more humble than other officers; it made him more daring. With so little to lose, Grant took more chances during combat than did a colleague like George McClellan, who had enjoyed so much success before the war that he had a lot to lose.

The greatness of many presidents was built on a foundation of being not so great early on. Before Valley Forge, Washington had failed repeatedly as a military officer and did a so-so job of running his plantation. Lincoln suffered multiple setbacks in business and politics. Franklin Roosevelt—a mama's boy and a mediocre student—was generally considered a lightweight before he moved into the White House. It's taken for granted by historians that, if he hadn't been paralyzed as a young man, Roosevelt would never have developed the grit, depth, and empathy he needed to become one of our best presidents. FDR's successor Harry Truman—today ranked by historians as one of our top half-dozen chief executives—didn't go to college, was an average farmer, and a failed haberdasher. "Most of our better presidents," Ronald Reagan assistant John Sears wrote in *New York* magazine, "learned to empathize through suffering personal tragedy or failure. . . . There is something about losing and coming back from it that burns character into a man's soul, breeds confidence without arrogance, and makes a man believable when he talks about problems. . . ."

Employees do better when they know they're being supervised by a human being, not someone merely managing them. This doesn't mean they spurn self-confident leaders who are in control of themselves. Mystique matters. We all want to believe that our leaders have exceptional qualities, but sometimes we want a bit of the opposite as well. At those times, an inscrutable mask makes it harder to lead. Both mystique and transparency are important for leaders and organizations alike.

Sharing

In today's economy, information is better shared than hoarded. That's a hard concept for many managers to accept. Consultants find that one of the biggest challenges in helping older companies get in shape for the twenty-first century is persuading them to loosen their grip on information once considered *proprietary,* protected not just from actual competitors but from colleagues jostling for position. New developments in business emerge so quickly now that struggling to keep a lid on information slows this process down. Secrets don't have the value they once had, and are seldom confidential, anyway. In the age of the Internet, hiding data is virtually impossible. Trying to do so hinders the marketplace for ideas that characterizes genuinely innovative companies, and wastes energy that might better have gone into innovating.

Hypersecrecy is a result of competitiveness run amok. No better illustration exists of the price companies pay for clinging to obsolete notions of success and failure. These notions are a product of overemphasis on competition. The idea that achievement is maximized when we go at each other hammer and tongs is engraved on our national psyche. When the road to success requires making others fail, however, innovation is hindered. Fresh thinking is more likely to result from collaboration than competition. Competition based on antiquated notions of success and failure segues easily into conflict, turning colleagues into foes. It infects coworkers with a desire to *win,* rather than to solve problems and move projects forward. In the process, they inhibit the free flow of information that's so vital to innovation. Those who feel that their work is being judged on conventional concepts of success and failure, and who feel as though they're competing with coworkers for the brass ring of success, will want to protect data rather than share it. This is a textbook way to squelch innovation. Their companies are the losers. If

Spencer Silver had thought it prudent to conceal information about his adhesive blunder, Post-it Notes might never have been invented.

Prizes for performance are especially effective at undermining teamwork by placing competition above collaboration. A food-services company we'll call Comestible created a contest to reward regional offices with the best sales record. Those who won got free vacation trips. This competition produced a few happy "winners" and lots of disgruntled "losers." Far from raising morale, the contest lowered it. *Winning* became such a fetish that Comestible employees began hoarding information that they might otherwise have shared with each other. Some even fudged their figures to get an edge. Comestible's motivational program had the opposite effect of that intended. Rather than encourage innovation based on collaboration and information sharing, their contest created an atmosphere of competition that stifled creativity, openness, even honesty.

The idea that competition leads to achievement is so basic to our way of life that the possibility of shifting to a more cooperative approach seems remote. In organizations of the future, however, this shift will be essential. Future-minded organizations, such as Shell and Monsanto, developed work groups that emphasize collaboration. In such organizations, exchanging information becomes the norm, not hiding it, as so often happens in the heat of competition. 3M has encouraged idea sharing for decades, in coffee-and-doughnut skull sessions years ago (like the one at which Art Fry heard Spencer Silver discuss his not-sticky-enough glue) to today's more formal tech forums and in-house trade shows.

Collaboration is the actual road to innovation, not striving for advantage by undermining colleagues. Many of the most valuable, imaginative members of an organization are not especially competitive. They have little interest in *winning* as such. The very concept is foreign to them. Because they feel no need to "win" every exchange of ideas, these employees don't do well in gatherings of colleagues playing verbal king-of-the-mountain.

Such meetings resemble TV talk shows more than they do searches for synergy. Ideas are exchanged in much the same way that rivals debate during political campaigns. Comments by colleagues are not listened to, but considered a good opportunity to organize one's own thoughts. The idea is not so much to generate information as to score points. Group members try to go one up by subtly (or not so subtly) putting each other down. Too often, this works. Research has found that critics of new ideas are assumed to be smarter than advocates of those ideas. Being critical makes us look sharper than being positive. Our chances of looking intelligent are improved by making others look dumb. At what price, however? What helps competitive individuals in this case hurts the organization of which they're a part. Who wants to suggest, or support, a new idea if the most likely result is to be cut down?

One of the greatest Achilles' heels of IBM's old decision-making process was that it gave too many people an opportunity to say *yea* or *nay* to new ventures. In Big Blue's hypermacho culture, saying *nay* ("nonconcurring" in IBM-speak) produced greater prestige than saying *yea*. As Paul Carroll discovered in his research on the company, "IBMers were considered wimpy if they didn't say no at least a few times on each project . . . [they] 'escalated' their fights as far up the management chain as they could."

This is how the old model of success and failure corrodes organizational culture. In settings where competition—winning and losing—are the underlying goal of all activity, it could hardly be otherwise. A process in which one's own success is more likely when colleagues fail generates far more friction than fresh thought. Competition-based cultures are especially hard on new hires, introverts, minorities, women, loners, and those for whom English is a second language. It's difficult to exaggerate the stifling effect that competitive idea exchange can have on such employees. They are the very ones who might have invaluable innovative suggestions, if they could only get someone to listen to them.

One way in which new technology contributes to innovation is by facilitating idea sharing. In organizations of all kinds, e-mail and conferencing software have encouraged bottom–up decision making, loosened sticky spigots of information, and become an electronic suggestion box. Royal Dutch/Shell has discovered that some of its employees' most innovative proposals come via e-mail. IBM's rebirth as a more nimble, web-savvy company began when CEO Lou Gerstner invited employees at all levels to communicate with him by e-mail soon after he arrived in 1993. It did not take long for Gerstner to begin hearing about stalled projects and unsolved problems that were stuck in IBM's many corporate cobwebs. Electronic mail has potent bureaucracy-destroying powers. In Robert Shapiro's words, e-mail "just rips through hierarchy." Monsanto's reinvention via self-organized teams was facilitated by this medium, which made it easy for employees with common interests to find each other.

New communications technology is the ideal medium for creative people who might be shunned or perceived as losers in organizations that rely too much on face-to-face idea exchange. The Internet provides a cover for those who might otherwise have trouble belonging to an organization. Online, one's age, gender, ethnicity, physical appearance, or personality quirks no longer determine the reception of one's ideas. New communications technology helps organizations retain unconventional, creative employees who may be bad at office politics, and facilitates taking maximum advantage of their talents. When face-to-face meetings are necessary, however, it's possible to conduct them in a way that encourages a free exchange of ideas rather than guarded one-upmanship.

Barnraising

At Royal Dutch/Shell, innovation teams fielded suggestions e-mailed by fellow employees. Using a method devised by consultants from Gary Hamel's Strategos, these six-person GameChanger teams met weekly to assess ideas. As Hamel reported in *Leading the Revolution,* during their first two years of operation, they assessed 320 proposals. All were evaluated not just on the basis of what Shell stood to lose by pursuing the suggestion, but what it could lose by *not* doing so. Several significant innovations at Shell began in GameChanger meetings. Among the most striking discoveries of this process was how many good suggestions came from employees who weren't thought to have an innovative idea in their heads. It turned out most had never been asked for one.

The best way to achieve an open atmosphere in which ideas can be freely exchanged is not by looking for successes to compliment or failures to criticize, but by creating an open atmosphere in which both are evaluated similarly. Group discussions can be based on this fundamental idea. Leaders set ground rules that encourage understanding rather than judgment. They emphasize that a good idea is a good idea, whether it comes from Peter Drucker, the *Reader's Digest,* or an obnoxious coworker.

This approach blunts the group's natural disposition to squelch imaginative, though difficult, participants. Once that's accomplished, psychologist Michael Kahn suggests running meetings on a model that's both new and old. Kahn's model is akin to *barnraising*—the way that pioneers pitched in as a community to help each other build barns. In Kahn's groups, rather than use the comments of others as time to organize their own thoughts, or as targets of criticism to show how much smarter they are, members are encouraged to listen carefully to each person's idea, then add their thoughts to see if they can build that idea into a valuable contribution. Evaluation is postponed. Criticism seems out of place. In this atmosphere of exploration, group members search diligently for value in ideas that might otherwise have been discarded. And they learn that their ideas will receive the same treatment.

As with Shell's GameChanger groups and Monsanto's self-organizing teams, barnraising-style teams share ideas and catalyze the innovation process. A similar kind of gathering is known as a *community of practice,* small groups of employees within an organization who meet regularly to discuss common interests. The value of this process goes far beyond information exchange. Such gatherings are greenhouses of innovation. In the *Harvard Business Review,* management consultants Etienne Wenger and William Snyder called communities of practice "a petri dish for entrepreneurial insights." This process is similar to brainstorming: suspending judgment and allowing members to toss out ideas in an atmosphere of cooperation and support, rather than competition and criticism. Unlike a skunkworks, these groups are ad hoc gatherings of those who come from many different parts of an organization, and return there. Like squid ink, the attitudes they develop in their meetings can permeate an organization's culture as a whole, particularly attitudes of daring. As the member of one community of practice told Wenger and Snyder, "I took a risk because I was confident I had the backing of my community—and it paid off."

What's really going on in these groups is courage enhancement. Tempering their anxiety allows them to see new possibilities better, even ones that might seem obvious. As we've seen, nothing is harder to notice than what's right in front of us, especially when we're anxious. Employees who are consumed by negative emotions—those who feel worried, helpless, beleaguered, or powerless—literally can't see what's before their eyes. Managers who develop an atmosphere of safety put new glasses on everyone's emotional eyes. Given lots of green lights, employees all of a sudden feel secure enough to look around. This not only improves their vision, but makes possible the kind of radical innovation that comes from noticing the obvious.

Nothing undermines innovation more effectively than fear. By the same token, nothing encourages innovation better than finding ways to cope with fear. Real innovation is most likely to take place among those who aren't hamstrung by anxiety. Meeting with others in an accepting atmosphere is one way to do this, and is an unusually effective one. There are others. In order to manage innovation better, we must first understand why the fear of failure can be so paralyzing. This would seem to be obvious. It isn't.

8 · Fear Management

Why is the prospect of failure so frightening, that we can't risk failing even when we know that's the only real path to genuine success? Actually, it isn't failure itself that scares us most. What really makes our hearts thump and palms sweat is the prospect of being *seen* as a failure. We reveal ourselves more in adversity than triumph. Suppose onlookers don't like what they see? What if they find us laughable? Failure could make us look ridiculous. The safer course is not to act, or say anything out of the ordinary, and to focus on appearances more than outcomes.

The Underlying Fear

A fear of embarrassment drives more psychic engines than we'll ever realize. This is the dread that transcends most others: looking foolish. Getting egg on our face. Feeling humiliated. The fear of humiliation is the least understood, but most paralyzing, of all inhibitions. Why else would polls routinely confirm that the fear of giving a speech ranks well above the fear of dying?

It takes two (at least) to create embarrassment. Stubbing our toe doesn't concern us so much as getting laughed at while we hop about whimpering. Flubbing a speech before a mirror is a giggle. Stammering before an audience is a nightmare. We laugh after dropping the ball when playing catch with a friend. Should we drop one during a game, however, our thoughts turn to entering the witness protection program.

An exaggerated fear of looking foolish is actually a form of egotism; an adolescent conviction that others are paying as much attention to us as we're paying to ourselves. The truth is that others are seldom this interested in us. They're too concerned about *themselves.* They're worried that we might be laughing at them.

Over time most of us learn to live with our own flaws. We grow tolerant of the mistakes we invariably make. Nevertheless, horror remains about the prospect of putting those mistakes on display for others to see: coworkers, neighbors, fellow parishioners, and our brother-in-law in Topeka. Nothing does more to keep us from taking risks we might like to take than the fear of looking foolish.

Branch Rickey said that baseball players' fear of being humiliated was far greater than their fear of being injured. Their worst-case scenario was looking foolish in the eyes of teammates. The same thing is true in the military. Officers know that what keeps soldiers fighting when every nerve ending says "Run!" is that the fear of losing face among buddies transcends their fear of dying. "In this business," said astronaut Walter Cunningham, "it isn't uncommon to be less concerned about getting killed than about making an ass of yourself, especially in front of your peers."

The fear of looking foolish underlies more activities than we'll ever know. Market researchers established long ago that consumers are far more concerned about how buying a new product will make them look in the eyes of others than by the possible loss of money. Not that they admit this. Money could be our most taboo topic. Group-therapy leaders have a much harder time getting members to talk about how they're doing financially than how they're doing emotionally. Most of us would rather discuss our sex lives, our loneliness, or our fear of dying than reveal how much money we earn and owe. As a result, all manner of financial transactions are driven by the need to protect one's face more than one's resources. When *Esquire* magazine gave investment guru Andrew Tobias $10,000 to invest and then report how he had done, Tobias found the pressure far greater than he'd imagined. "Not because of the risk of loss," he told his readers. "I didn't care a damn about the *money*—but because of the risk of looking stupid."

A fear of looking foolish keeps us from painting the pictures we would like to paint, composing the poems, making the friends, courting the lovers, pursuing the jobs, starting the businesses. Those who know this, who can confront and transcend their fear of ridicule, are in an unusually strong position. They understand that their best shot at a big success lies in accepting its partnership with the risk of humiliating failure. Every path breaker has looked foolish, and been humiliated, yet society depends on them utterly. Consider Galileo, Freud, Seward and his Folly. All persevered in the face of crippling ridicule. We might not know today that peptic ulcers result more from bacteria than stress if gastroentorologist Barry Marshall hadn't been able to endure years of withering scorn from colleagues as he tested this hypothesis.

Only those who are willing to risk looking foolish can invent a breakthrough, give a speech, found a company, or stand up for a principle. That doesn't mean they conquer this fear. It may not be conquerable. Being afraid, however, even of humiliation, needn't mean they let that fear paralyze them. It could even become their ally. The playwright Arthur Miller once said that the best work we do is on the verge of embarrassing us, *always*. A sense of impending chagrin is like a divining rod. If we are able to endure its sting, the fear of looking foolish can point us toward grails of achievement that are reachable no other way. According to Netscape cocreator Marc Andreesen the freshness of an idea can be tested by how much ridicule it provokes. An idea that isn't ridiculed is probably stale. If too many people think your idea makes sense, a dozen like you are already developing that idea.

Those like Andreesen who transcend their fear of ridicule to achieve something significant learn to be amused by their own foolishness. In the process, they add a powerful arrow to their quiver. Surviving embarrassment—shame, even—can be oddly liberating. Although excruciating when it occurs, a sense of chagrin can unlock gates of inhibition and pretense. Afterward, the image one has tried so hard to maintain disappears, a new humility emerges, and one is free to take a fresh look at vexing problems. "I remember how ashamed I felt after my divorce," recalled a management consultant. "It was so painful. At the same time it was curiously freeing in the sense that I no longer needed to maintain the façade of our beautiful magazine-cover family."

A fear of looking foolish can never be conquered completely. Nor should it be. Someone without a trace of bashfulness would be a hard person to engage. Deep-down shyness is a secret most charismatic people share. (Their dynamism is partly an antidote to their shyness.) Without that sense they would be less human, and less charismatic. Concern about looking foolish is at the heart of shyness. Much as we want to reduce that concern, we wouldn't want to eliminate it. Nor would this be possible. The fear of embarrassment is too ingrained. Even though fear—innovation's enemy number one—can't be vanquished, it can help those who are in fear's thrall to understand that fear is normal, can't be eradicated, but can be made more manageable.

Making Friends with Fear

While filling out a questionnaire on risk taking, a start-up company owner ran his finger down a list of fear symptoms. This list included: stomach butterflies, goosebumps, sweaty palms, racing heart, and trouble sleeping. "Check, check, check," he murmured. The man looked puzzled. Finally he looked up and asked, "Is there any place to mark 'All of the above'?"

Like most business founders—and risk takers of all kinds—this entrepreneur was on familiar terms with fear. Yet he hadn't let fear stand in his way. He had started his company despite being scared, not because he wasn't.

It makes sense to assume that those who take big chances must be unusually self-confident. It's also wrong. That's not how it is at all. Bold, towering figures are no less afraid than anyone else. They just don't let fear immobilize them. "I'm totally insecure," Abercrombie & Fitch CEO Michael Jeffries once admitted, "constantly scared." Like Jeffries, a surprising number of prominent men and women have carried on in the face of near-crippling anxieties. Legendary football coach Bear Bryant often threw up before big games. So did Bill Russell, as did Sir Laurence Olivier before stage performances. Winston Churchill may have been one of history's greatest orators, but the stage fright he suffered his entire life made him rehearse his speeches obsessively before giving them.

Ronald Reagan is another figure of apparent aplomb who never conquered his speechmaking nerves. According to Reagan speechwriter Peggy Noonan, the real reason he told so many jokes at the outset of speeches was less to humor the audience and more to ease his own anxiety. After realizing this, Noonan grew intrigued by the notion that successful people are scaredy cats. As Noonan later wrote in *Good Housekeeping*, she once sat next to a prominent woman at a gathering of colleagues—high-powered professionals all. "Do you know what all these women have in common?" her companion asked. Noonan said she didn't.

"They're all scared."

"How so?" asked Noonan.

"We're all afraid," explained the woman. "That's the thing that unites truly successful people: fear, fear of failing, fear of criticism, fear of letting down the team in some way. That's why they try so hard, that's why they pay attention to detail and try to get every possible duck in a row. It's fear."

Fear is not something to conquer or even ignore. It's too valuable a commodity. We get scared for a reason. Fear is adaptive. It tells us when to be alert. Feeling afraid motivates us to build strong fortifications. Anxiety advises us to unite with others, form tribes, countries, and enterprises. If we didn't get anxious, we would have vanished as a species long ago. The dodo, after all, was an unusually self-confident bird. Fear is a gift to our spirits for the same reason pain is essential to our health: as a flashing red light, a warning to learn from the Boy Scouts and Be Prepared. Those who ignore that signal are people to avoid. "I do what I can to get away from those fellows who never get scared," said the Arctic explorer Peter Freuchen. "They are very dangerous men. They get you into all kinds of trouble—those fellows who are scared of nothing. They die soon. I am always scared."

The value of fear applies to individuals and organizations alike. Former T.G.I. Friday's head Daniel Scoggin thought the reason once-successful restaurants stumbled so routinely was that the restaurateur's initial fear of failure got replaced by confidence of success. In other words, too *little* fear set the enterprise up for a fall. As Scoggin told psychologist Steven Berglas, author of *The Success Syndrome,* this alternative was to guarantee apprehension by setting ever higher goals for everyone involved—including himself.

It's important to distinguish between toxic and nutritious fear. One inhibits, the other arouses. Ski instructors say fledgling skiers make the most progress when they're pushed outside their comfort zone, but not so far that they're scared off the slopes altogether. Similarly, studies have found that, up to a point, performers of all kind benefit from the *audience effect* of having others around to unnerve and arouse them.

In the end, it isn't fear's presence or its intensity that determines our ability to act when anxious. Rather, it's the approach we take toward feeling afraid. Faced with danger everyone recoils. That's natural. The more important question is, what do they do next? Those who are paralyzed by the thought of taking a chance see only peril in fear's crackling flames. They imagine themselves being burned at the stake and back off. Those who see energy in terror's heat convert fear into fuel. To them, it looks like an exciting bonfire. The critic Kenneth Burke thought great artists saw opportunity in anxious experiences that others found merely menacing. The same thing is probably true of standouts in any field.

An understandable trap is waiting for fear to subside before acting. It doesn't, won't, and shouldn't. Too much is accomplished by people who are scared. Trying to wait out one's anxieties or portage around them simply postpones the day when they must be confronted nose to nose. Then the question becomes: Do we or don't we have the courage to act? Courage isn't *lack* of fear, after all, it's the ability to carry on *despite* fear. General Omar Bradley called courage "the capacity to perform properly even when scared half to death."

Genuine risk takers not only have the guts to act in the face of harrowing apprehension, they know how to harness fear's energy. Far from fleeing fear, they court it. Fear is a compass that points them in the direction of interesting risks to take. Bold innovators come to accept that anxiety is their constant companion: a crazy uncle up in the attic who stomps about, rattles his chains, and creates a commotion. That uncle could be ignored if he weren't such a nuisance. Alternatively, he can be brought downstairs and made to earn his keep.

Putting Fear to Work

After thirty years in advertising, Edward A. McCabe, who originated successful ad campaigns for Volvo, Reebok, Nikon, and Frank Perdue, among others, left the agency he cofounded to take up auto racing and freelance writing. The prospect scared him. He liked that. Abject fear was something McCabe hadn't felt since he had started ascending his career ladder and the fear of failing was what he clung to for support. When founding his agency as a young man, McCabe thrived on apprehension. Fear was the fuel that drove his engine. "My personal adrenaline-soaked security blanket," McCabe called it in a *New York Times* essay. "Success robbed me of that. One day I realized I wasn't scared anymore. People work a lifetime to earn that comfort. Not me. For me, losing the fear was like unexpectedly hearing that an old friend had passed away." This sense of loss was what led McCabe to enter the eight-thousand-mile Paris-to-Dakar road rally and write a book about the experience. Then, in his early fifties, he founded another ad agency.

Fearing failure is not necessarily a bad thing. Excitement, after all, is the flip side of fear. Any ten year old rolling downhill on a skateboard knows that exhilaration is primarily fear transformed. One study of skydivers found that the more fearful they were when leaping from a plane, the more elated they felt when their feet touched the ground. Fear begins as a negative sensation, but can end on a positive note in the form of excitement, elation, exhilaration, euphoria, even ecstasy. Enthusiasm is a close cousin. So are intensity, and concentration. All are by-products of fear. "We're so used to hearing motivational speakers and psychologists warn us about the fear of failure, we're probably reluctant to acknowledge what a motivator fear is," observed former Auburn football coach Terry Bowden. According to Bowden, "Some of the most successful people in business and sports are pretty good at using fear to push themselves into working harder, preparing better, and, once they're in the heat of battle, to jump on every opportunity."

The late boxing manager Cus D'Amato used to tell his fighters that fear was their best friend. Boxers who weren't scared enough let their mind wander. An ability to pay full attention to the task at hand—any athlete's most precious asset—is enhanced by fear. The best athletes manipulate their fear, use it as a source of anticipation, vigilance, and focus. So do the boldest people of all kinds. Whether it is the physical jeopardy encountered by a boxer, the economic risk taken by a business founder, or the social fears faced by a public speaker, heightened concentration is fear's most valuable by-product.

Sometimes speakers get on a roll and feel like athletes in the zone. The audience is completely with them. They're getting nothing but green lights. This shift from harrowing fear to total rapport can be so sudden and so complete that it defies explanation. Listeners seldom realize how frightened a speaker may have been before stepping up to the lectern. Experienced speakers worry if they're not anxious *enough* before a speech. Then their energy isn't fully mobilized; they lack the intensity that grows out of anxiety. Stage fright forces them to defuse their jitters with humor and banter. Most learn how to put both themselves, and their listeners, at ease with warm-up asides, particularly ones at their own expense. Antsy speakers often find themselves funnier than they thought they were. They say things they didn't even realize they knew. Elevated by their nerves, they become more witty and more revealing than they were when at ease. A too-polished performance may not be as effective as one in which ideas slip unexpectedly out of an anxious speaker's mouth. This can intrigue speakers as much as it does their listeners and allows them to connect better. None of this would happen if they weren't nervous before starting to speak, and didn't learn how to put their nervousness to work.

Performers of all kinds and at every level are energized by their fear of confronting an audience. They convert that fear to energy and focus. Luciano Pavarotti said it was *concentration,* more than voice, that made a singer great. Concentration is a response to fear. This was why, said Pavarotti, "I like 'nervous' in a performance." The secret of success, he concluded, was to be constantly scared.

When not a paralyzer, fear, even the fear of humiliation, can be a motivator. We're too quick to assume that fear leads to failure. High achievers don't see it that way. They see fear as a necessary evil at worst, at best, a valuable ally. Top athletes and coaches are circumspect about feeling afraid. In fact, they're circumspect about a lot more things than we think they are, including winning and losing, victory and defeat, success and failure. Like samurai warriors, they know that their best prospect for success comes in not trying too hard to succeed.

9 · Samurai Success

John Wooden's basketball teams won an unprecedented ten NCAA titles, including seven in a row. During his twenty-seven years at UCLA, Wooden never had a losing season. In one four-season span his teams won eighty-eight straight games. No other coach has come close to matching that record. None ever may.

To achieve this phenomenal record, one would imagine John Wooden put a lot of emphasis on winning. Actually, it was the other way around. UCLA's coach emphasized to all his teams, and to every player, that victory was not their goal. "Did I win? Did I lose? Those are the wrong questions," said Wooden. "The correct question is: Did I make my best effort? That's what matters. The rest just gets in the way."

According to Wooden, winning and losing aren't all they're cracked up to be, but the trip to that destination is. He felt that one's journey, the preparation to play, is what really matters. A game's outcome is simply a by-product. Getting there is where real accomplishment lay. All else is out of a team's hands. "I understood that ultimately the winning or losing may not be under my control," the coach wrote in *Wooden*. "What was under my control was how I prepared myself and our team. I judged my success, my 'winning' on that. . . . I felt if we prepared fully we would do just fine. If we won, great; frosting on the cake. But, at no time did I consider winning to be the cake."

116

Winning Isn't Anything

Our stereotype of top coaches is that they're obsessed, win-at-any-price types. That's certainly true of some. The real greats— the ones who enjoy success throughout their career, not just for a season or two—never made winning their goal as such. They include John Wooden, Dean Smith, Joe Paterno, and Vince Lombardi. Vince Lombardi? Mr. Winning Is the Only Thing? Lombardi's take on winning and losing was actually more complicated than that. Early in his career, like many colleagues, Vince Lombardi did say that winning wasn't everything, it was the only thing. He later revised his views, however, to say that the *will* to win was everything, a very different breed of cat. In a book published after his 1970 death, Lombardi wrote, "I have been quoted as saying, 'Winning is the only thing.' That's a little out of context. What I said is that 'Winning is not everything—but making the effort to win is.'"

This version reflected Lombardi's mature philosophy better than the one for which he's remembered. Lombardi was too shrewd a coach and armchair psychologist to emphasize winning per se. Yet, like most coaches, he knew how important that emphasis was to fans and owners, and alumni. Like his coaching colleagues, Lombardi also knew that losing was as much a part of success as winning. "If you can't accept losing, you can't win," he once said. The game was what mattered most, however; getting to stay in the game. Only winning would allow that. Victory was the means, not the end. Playing was the end.

Athletes have a saying: You compete to win, but you win to compete. As with gamblers, they understand that the best thing about winning is that you get to keep playing. Players in the emerging economy have a similar attitude. They measure their success by how long they can stay in the game. One computer engineer compared this process to playing pinball: "If you win, you get to do it again." Getting to do it again is the real reward, not some fleeting sense of victory.

Sport psychologists warn about the dangers of overemphasizing victory. Sometimes athletes need to be pumped up, they say. More often they're pumped enough, too tense about the outcome of a contest. This is especially true in playoff situations. Then, players need to relax. Wisdom comes in knowing when to give a pep talk, when to take a break. The best athletes learn how to relax themselves. They empty their minds before a tense contest begins, or visualize the moves they want to make. What they don't do is think about winning. "I never go into competition thinking I have to win," said Olympic gold medalist Kristi Yamaguchi. "That distracts me from skating."

Stressing winning inhibits daring. Those who take genuine risks know that failure is the norm, success the exception. This breeds a sort of blissful ignorance about the consequences of defeat. Winners know they must lose. They're good at losing. This doesn't make them good losers, or losers of any kind. They are people who know how to deal with defeat, and not let it devastate them. An ability to cope with setbacks is one of an athlete's most precious assets. When asked why he hired so many ex-athletes, an investment banker explained that it was because "they recycle so quickly after things go wrong."

An exaggerated fear of losing is the ugly sibling of an overemphasis on winning. Both cloud the mind. Psychologists have found that those who are terrified of failing when a situation calls for action are likely to either play it safe or take wild gambles. As an experiment, a group of children were given a competitive game to play in the presence of their parents (who were the actual subjects of study). The players most urged to victory by fathers and mothers proved to be most cautious. Those whose parents cheered but didn't push them were the ones most likely to take chances—and win. Not surprisingly, an American Management Association study of female business owners found that most came from families that stood by them, win or lose, and said so. These women became latterday samurai.

Zen Warriors

We know that the samurai were fierce warriors. What's less well known is how much their warrior ways were based on achieving victory by avoiding thoughts of victory. They knew that focusing on the outcome of a contest made defeat more likely. Samurai warriors too preoccupied by thinking about winning were likely to be vanquished by foes who simply concentrated on making their moves.

This attitude grew out of Zen Buddhism, which became central to the samurai creed after making its way from China to Japan in the thirteenth century. Thomas Cleary pointed out in *The Japanese Art of War* that samurai warriors were so captivated by Zen's emphasis on meditation, stoicism, and detachment—*emptying the mind*—that Zen became known as "the religion of the samurai." At the heart of its influence was an emphasis on achieving one's goal by ignoring one's goal. When it came to warfare, the samurai strived to achieve victory by becoming fully absorbed in a process that would lead them there, not by setting their sights on victory itself. The important thing was to be completely immersed in any activity, including combat. Samurai swordsman Miyamoto Musashi called this "total absorption of purpose in a single telling blow."

Total absorption of purpose, the samurai thought, made it possible for them to deflect a sword's blow with even a stick. By interfering with their concentration, thoughts of winning made it harder to achieve the complete concentration that allowed them to defeat a foe. Thoughts of any kind—about an opponent's sword, their own sword, killing an opponent, not getting killed by him—distracted a samurai from the task at hand. As master swordsman Yagyu Munenori wrote in a treatise on the art of war, "[S]uppose you are shooting and you think you're shooting while you're shooting, then the aim of your bow will be inconsistent and unsteady. When you wield a sword, if you are conscious of wielding a sword, your offense will be unstable. . . . When an archer forgets consciousness of shooting, and shoots in a normal frame of mind, as if unoccupied, the bow will be steady. When using a sword or riding a horse as well, you don't 'wield a sword' or 'ride a horse.' . . . When you do everything in the normal state of mind, as it is when totally unoccupied, then everything goes smoothly and easily. . . . When you are not consciously mindful, you'll succeed every time."

Samurai teachings have application far beyond swordplay, and well past their era. Today's best leaders are like outstanding samurai warriors in the sense that they engage themselves fully in tasks at hand without being distracted by what might go wrong. Warren Bennis called this *The Wallenda Factor*—putting one's energy into walking life's various wires without concern about the outcome. (The 1978 wirewalk in which the great Karl Wallenda fell to his death was the only one in which he focused on *not falling,* said his widow, rather than on simply walking the wire.) Like successful wirewalkers, effective leaders focus on tasks at hand, Bennis concluded, and don't let the possibility of failure break their concentration.

Great achievers of all kinds don't dwell on success or failure. They're too consumed by what they're doing to be distracted by thoughts of possible outcomes, positive or negative. Like the Wallendas and the samurai, they grasp the paradox that we're most likely to achieve a goal by becoming so immersed in an activity that we lose sight of that goal.

Pursuing a goal is usually more thrilling than attaining it: love interests, mountaintops, championships. The chase is the thing, win or lose. John Wooden said that this was a quality he observed in top athletes and businesspeople alike: "Both love the battle, the journey, the challenge. Both of them consider the final outcome a by-product." Though one might imagine that this upright attitude was a relic of Wooden's prewar Midwestern heritage, consider the most successful basketball coach of modern times: Phil Jackson. Jackson is Wooden's heir not only in an unbroken record of success but in the philosophy he developed to achieve it.

Jackson's Way

As a college basketball player and young pro, Phil Jackson was so consumed by the need to *win* that he didn't enjoy playing. Only after returning to his Christian roots, studying Native American religions, and taking part in Zen meditation did Jackson come to see winning as beside the point. His goal then shifted to being fully *present* in any activity he cared about, regardless of the outcome. Jackson called this process *mindfulness:* "simply paying attention to what's actually happening." He preached that philosophy to every player he coached. On and off the basketball court, Jackson told them, "Success comes from being awake, aware, and in tune with others."

By adopting this stance, Jackson's players, including Michael Jordan, Kobe Bryant, and Shaquille O'Neal, not only played together better, but won more basketball games. Jackson himself became the NBA's winningest modern coach. "Winning is important to me," the new Phil Jackson wrote in *Sacred Hoops,* "but what brings me real joy is the experience of being fully engaged in whatever I'm doing."

As Jackson came to understand, some things can't always be achieved by trying. Winning is one. Sincerity is another. So is joy. Vulnerability. Getting an erection. Getting pregnant. Trying too hard undermines all such achievements. Success, too, is something that can't be pursued directly. Success is a by-product. It rewards a job well done, a goal diligently pursued. But success can no more be obtained by pursuing it headlong than happiness can be achieved by grinning. Success is a reward for taking chances and doing a job well, not for doing a good job of pursuing success. Making an icon of success trivializes this concept. Setting out to be successful makes us less engaged in what we're actually doing. When too focused on succeeding, we're prone to avoid doing anything that might make us stumble. Yet stumbling could be a better method to achieve something big than striding smoothly toward a goal that keeps vanishing on the horizon.

No Regrets

When doing something we're passionate about, failure becomes a nonissue. Even our worst blunders don't feel like mistakes when they're a result of taking chances we wanted to take. The biggest regrets in life are for risks we didn't take, not ones we took and lost.

Pursuit of a dream rarely leads to regret—win, lose, or draw. *Not* pursuing one routinely does. A study of forty-eight women, ages twenty-five to sixty-seven, found that the happiest ones were fulfilling a childhood ambition. Those who weren't doing what they had dreamed of doing, no matter how successful they were in careers and marriages, invariably wished they had chased their dream instead. According to psychologist Patricia Weenolsen, who conducted this study, "Decisions of the head rather than the heart are the ones we most deeply regret."

Too many of those with unrealized aspirations have set them aside due to fear of failure. The bigger the dream, the greater the fear. Doing less than our best allays this fear. *I could have done better if I'd really tried,* we assure ourselves. Among the least appreciated reasons for doing superficial, second-rate work of any kind is the comfort of knowing it's not our best that's on the line. By not trying too hard, we avoid learning what our true potential is, and having to fulfill it. Doing our best can be deeply threatening. It forces us to consider what we're actually capable of accomplishing. Once we learn that lesson, we can't unlearn it. Our true potential becomes both a shining light we can follow *and* an oppressive burden of expectation that might, or might not, be met.

A fear of doing our best, of *being* our best, is one to which everyone is prey. In its clutches we may not succeed, but at least we don't fail. How could we? We didn't even try. Far more is at stake when we do what we *really* want to do rather than something less. We may never fully appreciate the role that not pursuing a dream plays in limiting people to disappointing careers and regret-filled lives.

Consider a retired secretary we'll call Emily. Emily led a supremely cautious life. Her reflex response to any suggestion for change was "No." Emily never married, didn't go to college, and lived in her parents' Chicago home. Her entire career was spent working in the same hospital. Emily had few actions to regret, because she initiated few acts. Her life was devoted to avoiding failure. As a result—in her own mind, anyway—Emily's life overall was one big failure. She entered the home stretch of that life filled with anguish about not having been bolder. In her late seventies, Emily observed that if she ever wrote a book, it would be titled *The Risks I Never Took*. We all could contribute a chapter to Emily's book.

Not taking more chances is a major source of regret. That may not become apparent until late in our lives as we review the many roads not taken. "I used to be so gutsy," is a common refrain. "What happened?" Such a realization doesn't necessarily lead to bolder living. Anticipating the pain of failure, at every stage of life we're all susceptible to avoiding activities that might fail. But failure's pain subsides faster than the ache of regret. Thoughts persist about what-ifs and what-might-have-beens had we been more daring. In the long run, avoiding activity that might hurt causes more agony than acting, failing, and dealing with the pain.

Failed risks at least leave us with the pride of having dared, and the knowledge that we gave all we had. A Philadelphia paper-goods salesman recalled wistfully the four years he spent in Los Angeles trying unsuccessfully to become a stand-up comedian. Did he regret the way things worked out? "Not a bit," said the salesman. "I gave it my best shot. Knowing that, I'm not unhappy with my life now. I'd only be unhappy if I hadn't tried to do stand-up first."

Risk takers ranging from entertainers through rock climbers to business founders seldom regret their daring ventures, even ones that go belly up. They know that few things are more satisfying than jumping high, even when they land on their backsides. Bold acts are rarely regretted, regardless of the outcome. On the other hand, obsessive brooding is often a result of throwing one's hand in too soon. Regrets bordering on mourning are felt about risks not taken: job offers spurned, loves abandoned, fights backed away from, pictures not painted, start-ups not started. Remorse is far more likely about being too cautious than about being too reckless. "I think I don't regret a single 'excess' of my responsive youth," said Henry James, " . . . I only regret, in my chilled age, certain occasions and possibilities I didn't embrace."

How Do You Measure Success?

As we've seen throughout this book, *success* is an elusive concept. Its definition varies with each individual, and changes with time and circumstances. That's why we so commonly fall back on wealth, awards, and talk-show appearances as the best measures of achievement. Inner criteria are more subjective (which is one reason they're paid so little heed). Yet the more we succeed on worldly terms, the more out of synch we may feel with our own values. Winning laurels of success has little to do with an inner sense of worth, and may even corrode it, as the gap grows between who laurel winners know they are and who the public imagines them to be.

Genuine success is not a state but a process. Never quite becoming the person we set out to be is inevitable, and not undesirable. Achievement elevates our vision. The bar always rises. What appears to be a success usually represents a plateau that's followed by new hopes, new expectations, and new frustrations, as our reach exceeds our grasp. Professional standing in any field is always tenuous. Earning lots of money usually makes us want to earn a lot more. Divorces are less likely to be sought by those in bad marriages than those in good ones who think they can do better. There is no lasting state of success. It is a target in perpetual motion.

The great irony of life is that achievement on the world's terms usually comes at the expense of contentment. Some do enjoy the rich satisfaction of a life they consider successful overall. This life might include a satisfying marriage, financial security, high professional standing, and durable friendships. Those who enjoy such a life have usually won success on inner more than outer terms. Life's most satisfying achievements may not even be recognized by others because they have no public or financial dimension. Getting your children to sleep, obtaining a yearned-for date, solving a knotty problem at work, building an addition to a house, learning to play guitar, or noticing guests you seated together having a lively conversation. Such accomplishments don't win plaques or bonuses. Yet all are rewarded by warm, private feelings of accomplishment, the satisfaction of a job well done.

Perhaps the most profound successes are those that would be gratifying even if no one else knew about them. One definition of maturity is the ability to keep feelings of accomplishment private. John Wooden said that long before he won unprecedented public acclaim as a coach he already knew he had put forth his maximum effort. That was why his ten national titles did little to validate his efforts as a coach, or add to his peace of mind. "That I already had," Wooden explained. "I had succeeded long before I was called a success."

In a celebrity-consumed era, it's easy to confuse fame with success. Our media provides us with a constant parade of outsize figures to whom we can compare ourselves. Their lives can seem so glamorous compared to ours. Why are they in Cannes when I'm in Canton? Celebrities have their own reasons to feel inadequate, however, and their own benchmarks to whom they compare themselves unfavorably. It could even be us. While we may wish we could join them at the film festival in Cannes, they might long for a kids' soccer tournament to attend in Canton, or a spouse who's happy to see them walk through the door.

Everyone has his or her own sense of failure. Fame is no antidote. Late in life, especially, setbacks tend to crowd successes out of memory. That's exactly what happened to J. Paul Getty. By most measures Getty was a smash success. He was among the world's richest men, squired some of its most attractive women, and assembled one of history's great art collections. The publisher of a book by Getty called him "the most success-ful man in the world." That wasn't how Getty saw himself. Quite the contrary. Toward the end of his life the oft-married oil magnate said "I hate to be a failure." J. Paul Getty? A failure? In what sense? "I hate and regret the failure of my marriages," he explained. "I would give all my millions for just one lasting mar-ital success."

Success? Failure? It's not always easy to say. These two can be hard to distinguish from each other at the time they occur. We may not even know until late in life, if ever, where we actually succeeded, and where we didn't. The business deal that seemed such a triumph at the time may be hard to recall when we're still sorry we missed our daughter's fifth birthday to negotiate that deal. Trophies on our mantle gather dust. Lasting friendships retain their luster. It may be up to our descendants to determine whether our life was a success, overall. We'd all rather find out while we're still alive. That's why the movie *It's a Wonderful Life* is such a lasting parable.

Beyond Success and Failure

There are many ways to define success—not just by fame and fortune but by a life well lived. Such a life goes beyond success and failure. Living this way is rooted in wisdom, in making sure that one's sense of self isn't too tied up with a defeat that could crush it, or a superficial victory that might lead to disillusion-ment. Both are handled with a similar posture: learning how not to be shattered by the humiliation of failure or unnerved by the stress of success.

In personal and professional lives alike, neither success nor failure is what it seems to be. This is our book's basic message. Success and failure can be hard to tell apart; one leads to the other and both have value. That conclusion has led to its most counterintuitive suggestion for leaders: Treat success and failure similarly, not with rewards or sanctions, but personal engagement. We have tried to show how many more management approaches become possible once conventional notions of success and failure are discarded. A both/and rather than either/or approach makes it easier to encourage inventiveness, support mavericks, do simultaneous planning, and destroy apparently successful businesses to make way for new ones that might fail— or win big. At the heart of this posture is greater acceptance of failure as a necessary part of innovation. This acceptance produces work environments that are genuinely risk friendly, which is to say, failure tolerant. Even though fear of failure cannot be eradicated from such environments, it can be managed, even put to work, as a source of energy and focus. Those who are passionately engaged in a task they care about are the ones most likely to achieve success, paradoxically, by minimizing thoughts of succeeding, or failing. This is the samurai way.

And, so, we come full circle. We began by saying success wasn't that different from failure. We end on that note, too. A genuinely successful life is most likely when we don't pursue success or avoid failure. We must go beyond those two impostors into a different realm altogether, where actual success is won by not seeking it, and failure managed by not avoiding it.